2001: A POETRY ODYSSEY
SOUTH ESSEX

Edited by Lucy Jeacock

First published in Great Britain in 2001 by
YOUNG WRITERS
Remus House,
Coltsfoot Drive,
Peterborough, PE2 9JX
Telephone (01733) 890066

HB ISBN 0 75432 430 3
SB ISBN 0 75432 431 1

FOREWORD

Young Writers was established in 1991 with the aim to promote creative writing in children, to make reading and writing poetry fun.

This year the 2001: A Poetry Odyssey competition again proved to be a tremendous success with over 50,000 entries received nationwide.

The amount of hard work and effort put into each entry impressed us all, and is reflective of the teaching skills in schools today.

The task of selecting poems for publication was a difficult one but nevertheless, an enjoyable experience. We hope you are as pleased with the final selection in *2001: A Poetry Odyssey South Essex* as we are.

CONTENTS

Gable Hall School

Gaynes School

The Poems

WINTER IS HERE

Sun shines on ice-covered streams
Turning things a shimmering gold
Children skating, wrapped up warm
Freezing earlobes hands protected from the cold

Jack Frost leaving sparkling trails
Glittering snowflakes floating down
Children's gleaming faces
A grey sheet growing across the town.

Ice-creamed colour faces
Shivering down the street
Doing their Christmas shopping
Wishing they were in the heat!

Redbreasted robin
Wonderful in its own way
White ghosts of trees
Winter is here upon this day.

Chelsey Dodkins (12)
Gable Hall School

ANIMALS AS I SEE THEM

Snails are very slow,
Cheetahs are very fast,
Dodos are extinct,
But elephants last.

Rabbits are very fluffy,
Snakes are very slimy,
Pigs are very fat,
Ants are very tiny.

Sharks are very scary,
Giraffes are very tall,
Stick insects are thin,
Ladybirds are small.

Spiders make me creep,
I don't like them at all.
Rabbits are my favourite,
I love them most of all.

Lauren Richards (12)
Gable Hall School

FRIENDS

Friends are important.
Without them I feel
Like a ball with no bounce,
A shoe with no heel.
Like snow with no flake
A real thing that's fake.

Friends are important.
They make me feel happy,
When I'm sad.
They make me feel good,
When things are bad.

Friends are important.
Treat them with care,
When you are in trouble,
They are always there.

Friends are important.

Katie Livermore (12)
Gable Hall School

FRIENDS

Friends are loyal,
Friends are true,
Friends are always good to you.

Friends are funny,
Friends are cool,
You can meet your friends at school.

Friends go out shopping with you,
And do other things you like to do.

Friends are there when you laugh and cry,
Doing their best, they'll always try.

All your life, you'll need friends,
Friends until the very end.

Leanne Jepson (12)
Gable Hall School

SWIMMING

Swimming, swimming
Is the best!
Far and wide,
Full with pride,
Up and down
As I frown.
Feeling dead,
I want my bed!
Another day at the pool
I must be some kind of fool.
To swim far and wide,
And still be full with pride!

Nia Gaut (12)
Gable Hall School

AFRAID OF CLOWNS

As they come into the ring,
and hit each other with pies,
and laugh when they squirt water into the audience's eyes,
I wish they would just go away,
and stop making me cry,
honking their red noses,
I wish that I could hide!

Jonathan Ford (13)
Gable Hall School

GRANDAD

My dear Grandad
Oh how I miss him
I loved him dearly
And now he is gone.

I miss his laugh
I miss his smile
I miss his silly stories.

He did all that four years ago
And now he is gone.

I begged and I cried
For him to come back
When I saw his flowers, his beautiful flowers
I couldn't even stand.
Mum said Nan would understand if I didn't want to come
But love my deepest love that filled my soul,
Stopped me crying and made me smile.

Emma Hill (15)
Gable Hall School

SMOKER'S PARADISE?

Smoking is bad for you,
It can cause all sorts of illness' like cancer.
My friends smoke.
I'm scared for them. What happens when they're old and ill
And can't eat without a tube in their throats?
They don't understand that I care for them so much.
They say I nag but they don't understand.
They don't understand
Sometimes they lie to me about it.
They say they've stopped.
I know they haven't.
I can smell it on them and when I ask they say I'm paranoid.
They don't understand I care.
They don't understand I love them.
They are my friends after all.
I wished they'd stop.

Amy Smith (14)
Gable Hall School

THE BREAK UP

When my mum and dad split up,
I didn't know whether to laugh, cry or scream.
I didn't want them to break up, but they said
'Don't worry dear, it's for the best.'

The family was no longer together,
I had lost my dad and I thought it would be
The end of the world.

I suffered the depression of losing my dad,
I got over the divorce and got through the arguing.

I stay with my dad at the weekends,
Sometimes I think I'm lucky, but other times I don't.

Now I know I'm not the only one who's lost their dad,
Now I know I feel great,
Because I know it's for the best.

Hayley Bigwood (11)
Gable Hall School

GUFFERY

On a spooky night in the middle of winter
There was a crack and a whack and a smack and a splinter
It was dark in the house with only a candle as a light
And Guffery the ghost was hiding just out of sight
As Jennifer Robinson walked through the door
Guffery the ghost knocked a book to the floor
Jennifer turned in fright, then suddenly stopped
When out of the wall the smirking ghost popped
She turned in a hurry and started to run
But she stumbled and tripped and fell on her bum
Then Guffery the ghost caught up right away
He said it's all right I just want to play
The ghost helped her up off the slippery floor
And they were the best of friends for evermore.

David Williams (12)
Gable Hall School

CHRISTMAS CAT

It was Christmas Day,
And my family had gone away.
I jumped up at the Christmas tree,
I know that was very naughty of me.
I heard the key turn in the door,
It was my family I was sure.
I wanted to run, I wanted to hide,
I wanted to be somewhere but not inside.
My family came in and smacked my bottom,
This is something I've never forgotten.
I went outside and began to cry,
I looked around and gave a sigh.
My owner came out and gave me a cuddle,
'It's alright,' she said, 'you just got in a muddle.'
I went back in and sat by the fire,
It was everything a cat could desire.

Heather Wallace (12)
Gable Hall School

THERE IS A HIPPO ON THE LOOSE!

There is a hippo on the loose!
He has escaped from the zoo.
He is getting into trouble,
By finding things to do.

There is a hippo on the loose!
He went into a mall,
He couldn't find the exit,
So he ran straight through a wall.

There is a hippo on the loose!
He ran onto a football pitch,
He didn't look where he was going
Then fell into a ditch.

There is no longer a hippo on the loose!
He is now back in his cage,
He looks so very angry,
In fact, he looks fuming with rage.

Mark Trunley (12)
Gable Hall School

SCARED

Scared of this,
Scared of that,
Some people are just
Scaredy cats.

Shaky legs
And shaky arms,
Wobbly knees
And sweaty palms.

Squiggly wiggly,
Queasy and squirm,
I really hate
Slimy worms.

Spiders, snakes,
I don't like,
They give all my friends
A big fright.

Scared of this,
Scared of that,
Some people are just
Scaredy cats.

Kristie Matthews (12)
Gable Hall School

MATES

My mates have a lot to do with my life,
Sometimes they are annoying like a nagging wife,
But when I'm upset and they comfort me,
Arguments are forgotten suddenly.

Problems are solved by me,
They talk and it sets them free.
Some days we go out
And most of the time we walk about.

When I don't mean to make them mad,
It makes me very sad.
I depend on them to make me better
And when I cry, they wipe away the tears which
                    make my face wetter and wetter.

I care for my mates, even if boys think it's slushy,
But one day they'll appreciate me being mushy.
Can they get annoyed? Yes they may,
Because it's all worth it at the end of the day.

Jennifer Ward (12)
Gable Hall School

SISTERS

Sisters,
Why are sisters so annoying?
They make you want to scream,
They think they can own you in every way,
They are so terribly mean.

They boss you about, 'do this, do that,'
They say it's because they're old,
They tell you to zip that big mouth shut,
'Just do what you are told!'

I can feel myself bubbling up with anger,
With every word they say,
You think to yourself 'Why me, why me?
Why don't you just go away?'

I don't think it's fair that us younger ones
Should put up with all this noise,
We should all go on one big strike for the day,
As my sisters weren't my choice.

Alex Gozna (12)
Gable Hall School

My Loss

As I sat in the empty room
Her voice echoed all around me.
My loss hit me as I touched her chair.

I remembered all the time we shared,
In the garden, watching television,
Drinking cups of tea.

I remembered her laugh, her smile,
The purple tint on her hair
As I sat there looking at her photograph.

I wondered where she was now.
I imagined her sitting with Grandad.
I realised my nan was gone
And I wasn't getting her back.

Natalie Smith (13)
Gable Hall School

MOTOR RACING

The smell of racing, the sweet, sweet smell,
The engines revving like a lion roaring,
The rush of racing is the only real drug,
The pleasure,
The excitement,
That's what makes racing so addictive.
The danger, people ask me
. . . I never think about the danger.

Rikki Taylor (13)
Gable Hall School

HALLOWE'EN

At the dead of night witches cackle,
A glowing gleam from the howling wolves,
Zombies rise from their graves,
Dripping fangs from vampires' mouths,
Devils scream at the light of fire.

Blood-dripping claws from werewolves of night,
Demons come with pumpkins alight,
Ghosts surround day and night,
Witches' spells with blood-curdling spiders,
Make this night a frightening remembrance.

Lauren Bell (14) & Danielle Barber (13)
Gable Hall School

FOOTBALL

Football is the game for me,
I play it always after tea,
Me and my mates, we argue a lot,
But like everything, there's always a plot.

We play a match on very Sunday,
Even if we lose, we still have a fun day,
We won the league and won the cup,
But soon I'll have to give it up.

David Salmon (13)
Gable Hall School

MY OLD RABBIT

I once had a guinea pig and rabbit,
They were getting on quite fine,
They shared a hutch together,
They were always kind.

All of a sudden my rabbit got myxomatosis,
Its eyes were all swollen,
Pus was coming out of his nose,
He was in real agony.

We had to take him to a vet.
She said he had myxomatosis,
There was nothing we could do,
We had to have him put down.

It was sad to see him go,
It was the only thing we could do,
It would be unfair to let him stay alive,
Because he would have died.

That's the tale of my old rabbit.
God bless, look after him.

Dean Craig (12)
Gable Hall School

CANDLE

The flame was flickering,
Wax was melting and running down the side.
It was orange-red in the middle.
Place was silent, still and pitch-black,
All you could see was this candle flickering.

Lauren Mobsby (13)
Gable Hall School

THE GALLOPS

The long, green stretch,
Waiting for us to come,
They're getting stronger,
Getting worked up,
Bouncing on the spot,
Then . . .
We let them go,
They gallop like the wind
Across the field,
Their tails flowing behind them,
The wind hitting us as we come to a halt.
Can't wait till tomorrow!

Laura McBride (13)
Gable Hall School

First Day At School

F irst I walked into my classroom,
I was very scared
R unning through the corridors,
S till very late,
T ime was going by.

D inner time was coming,
A fter lunch we were playing
Y o-yos were the 'in' thing

A nd everyone was happy.
T eachers rang the bell,

S chool had nearly finished,
C lasses were empty,
H omework had been set,
O ver to the car park,
O ver to meet my mum,
L eaving the car park to get home.

Abbie Allman (13)
Gable Hall School

HALLOWE'EN

October 31st, Hallowe'en is here,
People stay in, getting ready to fear
The ones who knock, 'Trick or treat?'
Holding out their hands wanting some sweets.
They are dressed as Frankenstein and Dracula.
To me, Hallowe'en is so spectacular.

Now it's my turn to dress up,
Quickly now, I'm going to erupt.
The excitement is taking over,
The green on my face, the colour of a clover.
These sweets I'm taking and some I'm robbing,
Have a guess what I am?
A grass-green goblin!

Thomas Turner (13)
Gable Hall School

SCIENCE FICTION

Welcome to the world of nothing,
Full of fear and action
With spine-chilling beasts,
Giving you nightmares of horror.
You know that it's terrifying and also fake,
This is science fiction.

Weird demons leave a big atmosphere,
With creepy, chilling features which make you panic.
Strange mis-creations leave you hair-raised the night after.
Going deeper and deeper into the world of eternal imagination,
This is science fiction.

Christopher Owen (14)
Gable Hall School

FRIDAY AFTER SCHOOL

On Friday after school I feel happy and excited,
I arrange to go out with my mates.
On Saturday morning I like to have a lay-in,
Then I get ready to go out.
We all go to town and have a great time,
Then we go back to someone's house.
We have a good day, and then it's time to go home.
I like to get my homework out of the way.

On Sunday morning I spend it all in bed,
I watch all my favourite TV programmes.
My mum always tells me to *'Get out of bed!'*
I finally get dressed and start my homework,
It takes me ages because sometimes I don't know what to do.
In the evening, I sit down and watch TV,
I get my bag ready for school.
At 10 o'clock I get into bed and fall asleep.

Lisa Addis (13)
Gable Hall School

FISHING

F inally the day has come,
I get there by car.
S eeing the mist hovering over the lake,
H earing the fish splash,
I know I'm in Heaven.
N o one there, silence is sweet,
G reat, I got a fish.

Martin Rivers (13)
Gable Hall School

CRAZY CLASSROOM

People running down the hall,
They don't have a care at all.
People drawing on the wall,
That's what happens at our school.

In the class we begin to play,
We usually do this every day.
We don't care either way,
And that is all we have to say!

Heather Wallace & Gina Mortlock (12)
Gable Hall School

BLAST OFF IN A ROCKET

Blast-off in a rocket,
Into space,
Wonder when I'll get back
From this massive, black place.

Blast-off in a rocket,
Up to Mars,
I met a green alien
So we sat and watched the stars.

Blast-off in a rocket,
Into a black hole,
There were no stars,
Just as black as coal.

Time to go home,
What a shame,
I saw a lot of wonderful things,
I'm so glad I came.

Ian Norris (12)
Gable Hall School

THE SKY

The sky is like an ocean,
Roaring when it rains,
Sparkling stars when the fish come out,
Twinkling my name.

The clouds are like boats,
Bobbing on the sea,
Floating in the air,
Wild, restless and free.

It's kept so very busy,
Holding things up high,
Helping the sun make the river glisten
And helping the wind sigh.

There's a galaxy beyond the sky,
Which is not that much bigger,
The Milky Way is its name,
With a lot of vigour.

Samira Abu-Helil (12)
Gable Hall School

DREAMS

Dreams are wonderful,
Magical things
With funny thoughts
And weird happenings.

Colourless but beautiful,
Strange but true,
Shimmering and shiny,
Only for your thoughts and
only for you.

Francesca Marzetti (13)
Gable Hall School

AUTUMN

Autumn is here,
Winter is near,
It is going to be a very cold year.

The leaves are coming off the trees,
Knocked off by the powerful breeze.

Brown, yellow, gold and red,
The leaves lie on the floor, crumpled up and dead.

The trees look all old and bare,
Brown and golden leaves are scattered everywhere.

Kirsty Mardle (12)
Gable Hall School

FRIENDS FOREVER!

I have a few friends,
Our friendship never ends,
We spend every day together.
Friends mean everything to me.

If our friendship ends,
My life will have no meaning,
You will have to scrape me off the ceiling.
Friends mean everything to me.

But luckily my friends aren't that out of order,
But they take the friendship to the border.
I'm glad to have friends like these,
Friends mean everything to me.

Gregory Starr & Robert Ramsay (13)
Gable Hall School

MY FAMILY

My family are, how you say, weird, completely bonkers.
My mum is this way-out hippy who
Believes in nothing but peace and love.

My grandad is this sixty-four year old who enjoys
Climbing mountains just for the fun of it,
Then there's little old me, the normal one of the family
Who has this silly ambition to become a psychologist, maybe.

I'm not really that normal, but
More responsible than the rest of my family.

My uncle is the manager of a car company
And at first sight he looks normal and responsible,
But then you get to know him and he
Eats, breathes and sleeps his band.

Then there's my nice little auntie,
She's just turned twenty-four.
She looks normal too, but you would be fooled,
She's a teacher . . . yuk!
So I've actually just proved that
All of my family are mad, including me.

Eden Robins (13)
Gable Hall School

MY MOTHER

Who is kind and caring,
has a heart of gold?
Sometimes moans,
but I still love her.

My mother.

Who has loved me and
my sister since we were little.
She cooks us dinner,
keeps us warm and gives us shelter.

My mother.

She teaches us right from wrong,
she takes us places, I am glad she had us
and I have never regretted it.
I am proud to be alive.
She is the fairy on the tree.

That's my mother.

Rikki Wilson (13)
Gable Hall School

GO NASCAR RACING

G entlemen, start your engines,
O n the starting lap, gather your nerves.

N on-contact racing makes it fun,
A rranging the grid then
S tart and the smell of rubber is like a blazing fire,
C ourageously going a few metres away from a concrete wall,
A ccuracy for pinpoint steering,
R unning in third place, working as hard as you can.

R acing past, the speed, the excitement, the danger,
A mazing racing for the crowd,
C oming in second place, catching up first,
I n the slipstream, speeding up,
N ow, go for a pass on the straight you do, yes you win.
G oing to Victory Lane, collecting the massive trophy.

Duncan Stone (13)
Gable Hall School

DISABLED

People are dumb,
People make fun,
I'm not dumb,
I'm normal.

They scream and shout, they always speak out,
I hurt inside, deep, deep inside,
I could cry, but I just sigh.
I'm not dumb, I'm normal.

I sit and think of all the good times,
They were so great,
It was when I had many mates,
They've all gone, I'm all alone.
I'm not dumb, I'm normal.

I dream of all the good times
And I cry for the bad,
It makes me mad when people stare,
I just give them a glare.
I'm not dumb, I'm normal.

People are dumb,
People make fun,
I'm not dumb,
I'm normal.

Kimberley Portas (16)
Gable Hall School

FIREWORKS

As high as a skyscraper,
As loud as a gun,
As bright as the sun,
Screaming through the air,
Blowing up in mid-air,
The smoke blows you out,
It could knock you to the floor.
Big ones to small ones,
They're all exciting,
But then the night ends,
It's time for bed.
'But Mum,'
'Bed.'

Daryl Martin (11)
Gable Hall School

SWIMMING IN THE SEA

It's good swimming in the sea,
The sea is very murky and sparkly.
You can swim in the sea for pleasure or just for fun.
If you like fish or coral, go scuba-diving.
The best place to go scuba-diving is Australia.
You can see all fish and coral there, it's great,
But a beach in England is good enough,
So try it.
Swim in the sea.
It's fun!

Joseph Smith (11)
Gable Hall School

DREAM AWAY

When the door closes the dream begins,
That's when the journey starts.
Light flashes and the corridor lengthens,
That's when your mind takes control.
Where does it go, when does it end,
That where your mind can flow?
Am I dead or am I alive?
That's when your mind takes to overdrive.
Wake up! Wake up!
That's when your mind comes alive!

Liam Beresford (14)
Gable Hall School

HARVEST

Harvest comes around,
it doesn't make a sound.
Crunch, crisp leaves on the floor,
flowers come and go
as the farmer starts to sow.

In the spring they start to grow,
all the animals are up on show,
as the birds start to tweet,
the farmer is cutting the wheat.
All the oats, barley and corn are done
and here is summer, here it comes.

Sarah Bates (11)
Gable Hall School

AUTUMN HAS COME

Leaves are falling all around,
Crunchy-crisp, that's their sound,
Brown and orange, sometimes red,
Some of them are already dead.
Animals hibernate, they go to sleep,
Birds are singing in the trees.
Weather turns cold, it gets frosty too,
I love autumn, do you?

Kirsty Deabill (11)
Gable Hall School

LOVE STINKS

Those subtle winks that the guy you fancy
sends to the blonde sitting next to you,
love stinks.

When you go home to get the biggest ice-cream tub
you can find and the guy you fancy comes and knocks
and tells you that those winks were for you,
love stinks.

Jenny Fletcher (11)
Gable Hall School

SUMMER

Summer is here. It's really hot!
The sun gets brighter every minute of the day,
people sunbathe and they're burnt already,
for the sun is so hot.
People queuing in cars to get to the beach.
Sandcastles everywhere, people are asleep,
for the sun is so hot.
The breeze moves in and the leaves start to fall,
as autumn creeps nearer, the sun starts to cool!

Olivia Leigh-Hudson (11)
Gable Hall School

THE BOY WHO COULDN'T READ

There was a boy called Thomas Mead
Who never, ever learned to read,
'I wish you would' his teacher sighed,
'Why should I?' Thomas Mead replied.

Well one day he went out walking
And heard the men above him talking,
But couldn't read the sign that said,
'Danger, workmen overhead.'

A pot of paint fell through the air
And changed the colour of his hair.
'Can't you read?' the workmen cried.
'Why should I?' Thomas Mead replied.

A lady said, 'What a disgrace.
Why don't you clean your hair and face.'
She pointed to a big glass door,
'There's a washroom in that store.'

He pushed the 'pull' sign on the door,
And knocked some shoppers to the floor.
'Can't you read?' the shoppers cried,
'Why should I?' Thomas Mead replied.

A trolley loaded to the brim,
Tipped its load all over him,
So Thomas thought he would leave the store
And ran downstairs to the door.

I think you should learn to read,
Thomas Mead.

Danny Sparks (11)
Gable Hall School

NIGHTLIFE

One, two, baby went to the loo,
Three, four, baby went some more.
Baby starts to whimper, baby starts to cry,
Wakes his mummy and daddy up,
Mummy gives a sigh.
'Your turn Daddy, I did it last.'
Daddy's not so sure about this, lazy old Mum.
Daddy takes the nappy off, drops it in the bin,
Puts a brand new clean one on
And tucks the baby in.
'Night, night baby, night, night son.'
Daddy back in bed again,
Three, two one.

Nathan Smith (11)
Gable Hall School

THE HARE AND THE TORTOISE

'Slow and steady wins the race.'
I'll get there in the end,
A few more yards, not far to go,
It's just around the bend.

Faster, faster
And faster still,
Hopping, haring
Over the hill.

Plodding along,
Slow in speed,
Look at the hare,
He's in the lead.

All this running
Makes me weary,
I'll have a nap
Cos he's not near me.

'Watch out hare,
I'm coming past,
You had your nap
So you're now last.'

Steady tortoise
Won the race,
Lazy hare
Took second place.

Nicola Watson (15)
Gaynes School

THE LAST SUPPER

What was that noise and the trembling deep in the ground?
I look through my window as I hear the bells clang.
It's not the church bells,
It isn't the rag and bone man,
I didn't want to hear but I knew it was the mine's bells.

There must be disaster,
I fear the truth.
My loved one is down there, deep in the mine.
Oh I hope he's not hurt!
I want my Tom back.

Hundreds of women all crying and screaming,
Running down the steep hill to the mines below.
I must go and join them,
To find out my fate,
To find my loved one, my darling Tom.

I remember last night, so near but so far,
As we sat together gazing deep into the fire.
We talked of our baby, yet to be born,
We talked of our future and ate our last supper.
No, it won't be our last, Tom will come back.

As Tom had stroked my rounding belly and the life which grew inside,
He told me he loved me,
He told me he would not leave,
So why do I fear as I remember his words?
'I will always be with you my darling young girl.'

It's a dank chill morning,
The mine spreads between us and our loved ones,
Fathers, sons, brothers and lovers.
We are there hoping for a miracle,
But fearing the worst, why should God care?

Hours pass before us,
The mine slumbers on,
Unwilling to free our men from its cold, dark heart,
Wanting our pain and sorrow,
A tribute for the gold which we have taken.

The second shift men have been digging,
Digging for life, not the empty dreams of gold.
I would give anything
To hold my Tom again and feel the joy of our soaring love.
His life is my greatest treasure.

The mine has come like a thief in the dark,
Taking my love, our beautiful love,
The spell has been broken,
It was to be forever,
There's no greater pain than the pain of goodbye.

The first men return from the deep below,
They are sad and look small.
Deep within the earth they have seen their death,
The bodies follow, so cold and so stiff.
And there is Tom, my darling Tom.

The tears will not come,
But deep within, my heart is breaking.
Our beloved baby kicks
And my soul shivers like a candle in the wind.
It was our last supper . . . Tom is no more.

Michelle Groom (16)
Gaynes School

HOPE

A flower,
A white flower,
An elite bud, poignant
Though draped in unclear mist.

Though confused by her loneliness,
She blossoms each day
To touch others in her life
With the joy that she craves.

Imprisoned in cold residence,
She has no fond memories of happier times,
For her household is bitter and indifferent
And her future is indistinct.

Yet, she is strong,
Her judgement remains unclouded
And she unfolds to face her icy world.

Jeni Beckett (15)
Gaynes School

CUP FINAL DAY

Three minutes to kick-off and the players were out,
the fans began to rave and shout.
The whistle went, the game began,
The national anthem's been sung.
Tackles went in as hard as nails,
the players were going wild, like doggies' tails.
A goal!
A crash of the drums,
a roar of the crowd,
the manager was really so very proud.
The half-time whistle sounded,
the players' tunnel got crowed.
The players could have a long rest, and there
was a half-time song with Georgie Best.

The second half has begun
and the team talk has been done.
The second half was end to end
and the tension was driving the fans round the bend.
The other team scored and the fans roared,
the score was now 1-1.
Two minutes from the end there was a quick attack,
a player was brought down like a heavy sack.
A penalty was given and the player scored
and the opposite team's fans' tears poured.
The time was up,
the home team had won,
it was time for them to lift the cup.

Daniel O'Driscoll (13)
Gaynes School

THE WOLF

Walking through the woods and
There I saw the storm.
A dark blanket of rain,
Crashing, tumbling,
Lighting the night sky.

A howl of a midnight wolf,
Claws scraping the ground,
The screams surround us.

Red eyes pierced the darkness,
Glittering in the moonlight
And there I saw the wolf,
Howling in the moonlight.

I could see the teeth,
Drips of blood,
Blood flowing to the ground.
Then he saw the sun
Breaking the cloud,
He ran into the darkness of the forest
And was never seen again.

Ross Cornwell & Sam Healy (12)
Gaynes School

LOVE

Love is a summer's day,
Comforting and warm,
A glow of sunshine.

Love is a child at play,
Oblivious to its surroundings,
Intense yet reckless.

Love is a sunset beach,
Waves clashing silently
Against the shining rocks.

Love is also hatred
Building up inside you,
Ready to explode.

Love is anger
Like the raging sea,
Violent and rigid.

Love is destroying,
Like a world war
Breaking up families.

Love is . . .
Heartbreaking.

Jade Halpin (13) & Heidi French (12)
Gaynes School

LOVE ON A SUMMER'S DAY

Love on a summer's day is like
Christmas treats,
joyful and warm.

Your heart is like
a snowflake,
so fragile and pretty.

You know you're falling in love
because your stomach's
full of butterflies,
flapping up and down.

Love you can treat like
anything you feel,
whether it's a good or bad feeling.

Love is something that
cannot be explained,
like a puzzled person not
knowing what to say.

Love is a time to be happy,
when there is someone
special in your life.

Jennifer Breden & Melissa Golden (12)
Gaynes School

THE OLD CARAVAN

The old caravan came crashing down
Like a tonne of bricks
But still landed as soft as a feather
As it fell all the way from Heaven
And it sits there
Like an old, rusty statue.

As the wind blew
The old caravan flew
Back a couple of miles
In the middle of an empty field
As the wind whistled wildly
And the birds sang so sweetly,
The old caravan sat there as still as could be.

Reice Black, Danny Lawrence & Mark Dicks (12)
Gaynes School

EIGHT DAYS A WEEK

Monday is the worst day of the week,
back to school,
homework an' all.

Tuesday is work day,
Mum ain't home,
microwave chips.

Wednesday is pay day,
all the new fashions,
on me.

Thursday is tongue-twister day,
me and my boyfriend Jay,
diamond on my finger,
'Get your money out Jay,
I ain't paying for anything till pay day.'

Friday is end of school,
dumped Jay and I'm two-timing Paul,
shall I tell him when I get back to school?
No!

Saturday is hangover day,
too many drinks,
I fell like a tornado on the go.

Sunday is accident day,
Smash!
There goes my cup of tea.

Relax day is no hassle,
my bones feel like they are the wind,
the air is so hot,
my hair feels like raindrops dripping down my face,
the sun's gone down
and the moon's come up.
Goodnight, God bless!

Danielle Chapman & Faye Knowles (12)
Gaynes School

RAINY DAYS

'It's raining out,' said Mum to me,
'So don't forget your hat,
You're going to need your wellies too,
You can't go out like that.'

I put my hat and wellies on and went out in the rain,
I went through puddles big and small
That I found down in the lane.
I went and shook the holly bush,
It dripped all over me,
I chased a frog down by the pond
Then I went home for tea.

'Just look at you,' said Mum to me
'You've ruined your nice new hat
And got your wellies soaking wet,
You can't come in like that!'

Sîan Cousins, Carly Hipson (12) & Kayleigh Heagren (13)
Gaynes School

MILLENNIUM

Two hours to go till the Year 2000,
Everyone waits
Lovely, loudly, lively,
Crowding the Millennium Dome,
People wait for the clock to strike 12 o'clock.

One hour to go till the Year 2000,
Screaming, shouting, swearing,
Saying silly things,
London is as busy as a theme park,
Waiting to go in.

Two minutes to go till the Year 2000,
Party poppers ready,
People waiting, silently,
For Big Ben to strike.

London is as still as glass,
Suddenly the city is alight,
Bang! Bang! Bang!
The Year 2000 is here.

Sarah Butler & Amy Beardsell (12)
Gaynes School

FALLING IN LOVE

I met this boy at school,
He really is quite cute
And when I talk to him,
I think we sort of suit.

He has eyes the colour of grass
And his hair is super blond,
I suppose you could say he's a bit like me,
Like I said before, we bond.

Philippa Barnes (13)
Gaynes School

LOVE

Since you went away,
I've been missing you so,
I can't get to sleep at night,
There's just one thing I need you to know.
I will always love you
From the bottom of my heart,
You're always in my memories,
Even though we're apart.
Our love was like a starlit sky
That twinkled high above,
But since you went away I see
That I am truly in love!
The tears I cry for you at night
I know are just a waste of time,
I wish I'd never laid eyes on you,
This feels just like a love crime.

Justine Rigden & Kim Gilmartin (13)
Gaynes School

PERSONAL EDUCATION

PE can hold some great sports,
The memorable three-pointer in basketball,
The one great goal in football
Feels like a lion after catching its prey.
The superb four in cricket
Is like no other feeling.
The *bang* of a rugby tackle,
The glory of a try.
The match points in badminton
Feel like your first kiss.
To win a hockey match,
It feels so good.
Silly Sam scoring a great goal,
The smiles on everybody's faces
When their team scores a goal.
All the great games, but the best?
Nobody knows.

Jed Connelly & Jonathan Barnes (13)
Gaynes School

GOING FOR GOLD

They train and train all day long,
But it is worth it when the Olympics are on.
The crowd is growing as the tickets are sold,
The runners are ready for that special gold.
They are fast,
They are slow,
On the track there they go.
Like a bullet out of a gun
They speed down the track,
Look at them run.
The excitement and the rage,
The winner will be on the front page.
They are on the final bend,
The race is coming to an end.
They look at the sky so blue,
Their dreams might all finally come true.
The lights, the cameras are coming round,
The crowd is like a lion, a roaring sound.
The winner takes the gold,
It is his forever to hold.

Steven Dennis (13)
Gaynes School

FOOTBALL, FOOTBALL

Football, football,
The food of love.
Better than chicken korma,
Better than Christmas pie.

Excited and in control,
Shooting, scoring, slicing the ball,
The net rips as the ball goes in,
Like a pair of trousers on a child
                    doing the splits.
A goal! *Hurray!*

Greg Armstrong (13)
Gaynes School

ANGRY MAN

Bang! The door slammed,
Angry man walked in.
Stamp, stamp! went his feet.
'I hate my life and my wife!
I scream and scream!
I plead and plead!
I never get what I want!
I'm hungry as a horse!
I'm wet as a fish!
Make me my dinner!
Run me a bath!
I am the Angry Man, you can't make me laugh!'

Thomas Andrews (13)
Gaynes School

CHRISTMAS POEM

'Ho, ho, ho!' goes Santa Claus
climbing down the chimney with his bag of toys,
getting them out for the good little girls and boys.
He looks at his list
to see who he had missed,
so he goes outside ready for his ride
with his red-nosed reindeer behind.
He couldn't believe the night was nearly through,
but he had a job to do.
He hopped on his sleigh and said 'Let's go!'
He went through the sky and shouted out
'Merry Christmas!'

Lauren Necati (13)
Gaynes School

School Bully

The sound of the bell,
The children run,
But I'm not having much fun.

They wait for me just after the bell,
Then they make my life hell.
They scream and shout and
Push me about.
They squeal like pigs and
Give me digs,
They push and pull in the school.
I cry for help but it never comes,
Then they run off to their mums.

Walking home through the park,
I don't like being alone in the dark.
There they wait
By the swings and call me names and
Start throwing things.
When I get home, my mum asks if I'm OK,
Then all I do is sit and pray.

Kirsty Gilmour & Melanie Foster (13)
Gaynes School

AEROPLANE

Taking off like an eagle,
Swooping like a bird,
Gliding like a swan,
Swaying like a sparrow,
Diving like a blackbird,
Landing like a butterfly.

Controls at my fingertips,
All the control in the world,
Images flashing by,
A roller-coaster ride.

Whirring, swooshing, humming,
Grinding, tumbling, scraping,
A fantastic machine
Of discovery.

Jonathan Bounds & Ryan Fowler (12)
Gaynes School

LOVE

Love is a feeling you get inside your tummy
And it feels quite funny.

It feels like butterflies,
Or it's a bird that flies.

When it's bad it can be heartbreaking
As it comes down with a *crash!*

With the exhilaration of love,
You feel like a bird.

Your heart a-flutter as
Your emotions loop, swoop and swerve.

In the end it ends in a big crash,
Like glass being smashed.

But not all love ends!

Grace Chapman & Emma Christmas (12)
Gaynes School

DAD, HE WOULDN'T WOULD HE?

It's nearly Christmas, I just can't wait,
I am going out with Dad, he's really great.
When he's at home, he's a good dad,
Everyone's happy and nobody's sad.

Everyone's perfect no lies can be seen,
No one knows what's under his sheen.
At the table eating food,
We're all quiet and not being rude.

He comes home with gifts and a flower,
He gives the family all of its power.
It's not normal, all of these things,
He's home later where has he been?

Mystery phone calls from someone strange,
He shrugs it off and makes a change.
The smell of perfume, lipstick on collar,
All of what he's saying is difficult to swallow.

I come home from school, everyone's sad,
What is happening, where is Dad?
I've just found out he's gone forever,
He did something stupid and not very clever.

It's a year since it happened, I cannot remember
What happened last year before September?
The tears that were shed, the anguish and pain,
I don't want to go through this *ever again!*

Kirby Stebbing (13)
Gaynes School

PAULA YATES' BALLAD

When Paula was young she was full of grief,
She turned her eye to fame.
She wasn't very happy,
Her heart was full of pain.

In 1986 she married a famous star,
They were the perfect couple,
Their marriage lasted a long time
But there was a sign of trouble.

The marriage finally ended with Bob,
But for Paula it ended in tears,
There was a battle over the children,
For the girls to be taken away, that was her fear.

Paula soon fell pregnant with Hutchence's baby,
She had another girl,
They were happy when the baby arrived,
And debated over calling her Tiger or Pearl.

In a Sydney hotel Hutchence felt sad,
That night tragedy hit,
He thought his life was hell,
So he decided to quit.

She soon got over Michael's death,
But now she was addicted to drugs.
She hung around with all the wrong people,
But she didn't realise they were all thugs.

All was quiet in the house,
Paula lay still on her bed.
Tiger Lily ran into her mummy's room but couldn't
                                        wake her up.

She was dead.

Lauren Stewart (13)
Gaynes School

THE BALLAD OF ROSE

Rose met two girls named Jean and Kellie,
She thought they were kind,
She lent them and gave them money,
Of course, she didn't mind.

Rose lived on her own in London,
In the war her friends died,
She missed them ever so much,
Although she survived.

The two sisters, Kellie and Jean,
Would often pop round,
Little did poor old Rose imagine,
She was in for a pound.

Rose had told them all her secrets
And where she kept her money,
They had an ideal of stealing it,
Thinking it would be funny.

The sisters knocked her to the ground
And left her for dead,
They took her life savings, £800,
Next, she was on her death bed.

They callously bragged to their mates,
But it was a crime,
One mate decided to tell the police,
They're now doing time.

'They should throw away the key,
After taking away my life.
Just look at what they did to me,
Please take away the strife.'

Hailey Dunne (14)
Gaynes School

A CRISP, COLD, WINTER'S DAY

Wrapped in a cocoon of clothes
I braved the elements.
The icy wind clawed its way through my body,
Stripping me to a mass of shivers.

The world glistened a shiny white,
Like icing on a cake.
My breath puffed in front of me,
Like water at the boil.

As I scuttled across the path,
It was like walking on a trail of crisps, crunching and crackling,
The cold gnawed at my fingers,
I couldn't wait to get home.

Andrew Meech (13)
Gaynes School

THEY SHOT MY BABY

There was a young girl named Sarah
Who was sitting in her father's car
When she heard shooting in the distance,
But not so far.

They can hear the shooting getting closer,
Sarah begins to cry,
Her dad stops the car,
Sarah gets a bullet in the eye.

Sarah's father shouts out 'No'
But it's too late,
Sarah is dead.
Open up heaven's gate.

People stand and watch
In utter disbelief,
While they hear orders
Given out by the chief.

They cover up Sarah's body,
Let her rest in peace,
But the shooting continues.
Will they ever cease?

It sees like no one cares,
They just stand and stare.
There's not place to hide
From what's really there.

Ashley Payne (13)
Gaynes School

TEENAGE SUICIDE

Young broken-hearted Jade Impson
Was brought to hospital last night.
The fourteen-year-old was in a severe coma,
It wasn't a pleasant sight.

She had found out where her dad was
After searching for a long time,
Four years of tracing,
It was a very steep climb.

Jade was only ten,
When she was told about her dad,
She went to visit the family
She was ever so glad.

But the message she got back
Was always the same,
Her dad had a new family
And couldn't take the pain.

She was going to shoot herself,
She swallowed some pills instead,
She took all eighty tablets,
Now the girl is dead.

Her mum was sitting there this morning,
Tearful beside her bed,
When the life support machine went off
She finally laid her head.

Her mum donated her organs
To save the life of others,
It filled her mother's heart with joy
To save the live of another.

Nick James (13)
Gaynes School

MICRO SCOOTER BOY!

Have we all heard of Arron,
He was a well-loved lad,
He was involved in a car accident
That everyone found sad.

It happened in the year two thousand,
In the month of September.
He was riding across the road,
Oh surely, you must remember.

He was riding one of those scooters
On a busy road in Anfield.
He didn't see the cab coming,
The poor lad got killed.

A garage worker was doing his work
When he heard a scream.
He dropped his spanner and ran out
And saw it wasn't a dream.

The ambulance came immediately,
But didn't get there quick enough,
They saw Arron lying there
And took it really tough.

The police phoned his parents
To tell them of their son,
Their voice broke down in sadness
About what the accident had done.

Karri Vallis (13)
Gaynes School

THE BALLAD OF PAULA YATES

At an early age
Paula Yates found fame,
But her life came to an end,
Just like all the same.

Tiger Lily lies dreaming
While Mummy lies still,
She wakes without noticing
Her mother is ill.

In early hours of Sunday,
Tiger Lily goes walking around the home,
Still her mother lies dead in her bed
While Tiger Lily cries down the phone.

The police and press come knocking,
But no one comes to the door,
They begin to panic and worry,
Paula is alive no more.

The young girl's tragedy
Affected us all,
But we know she's in good hands now
As she watches her children grow tall.

We give our hearts to Tiger,
Now she's all alone.
The thing we most remember
Is her crying down the phone.

Aimee Marshall (14)
Gaynes School

WINTER

Winter winds blow wildly,
Ice freezes on the lake,
The snow falls like flour
Being sprinkled on a cake.

Winter is when the earth is still,
Nothing moves when it's about.
Snowmen stand still and silent,
Like a child being shouted at.

Winter spreads across the land,
Sledges slide and snowballs fly away.
Ice creeps over the lakes,
Like a spider creeping towards its prey.

Soon the snow begins to melt
As quickly as a cheetah runs.
Finally the earth is warm again,
Like a fire glowing at night.

Kevin Smith (14)
Gaynes School

THE ATTACK

There was a man called Iannis,
To the town of Tilbury he came,
The twenty-three year old seaman
Was walking down Landsdown Lane.

On a summer's night in August,
He was senselessly abused
By a group of brainless hooligans
He was violently battered and bruised.

The police described it as violent,
He was lucky to be alive.
One month in hospital and unconscious for a week,
He was struggling to survive.

The seafarers helped in all kinds of ways,
Money and flowers for the family.
The local people supported him,
So he knows he is not lonely.

The family flew back home,
Iannis is struggling to talk.
He had a major operation,
But luckily he can still walk.

His father, Captain Tritsarolis,
Was extremely thankful
For all those people who helped him,
He couldn't be more grateful.

Asha Loganathan (13)
Gaynes School

THE BALLAD OF A HOLIDAY TRAGEDY

Jane Lilley sees off the big party
On their lovely evening cruise,
But as a storm suddenly blows up,
It ends up capsizing the crew.

The capsized boat drifts overnight
Towards the southern coast,
They failed to see the warning light
And hit the rocky coast.

The four survivors were plucked from the lake,
After they were spotted by a boat,
The man who saw the capsized boat was the first mate.

To survive a blast like that,
The four men were lucky,
But knew it was all in the past and that's that.

But now their loved ones are weeping,
Remembering the big blast
That killed their loved ones so fast.

Nicholas Power (13)
Gaynes School

DEATH TOLL RISES IN WEST BANK!

Twelve year old Rami Aldura
Was killed in Gaza today,
Caught up in the crossfire,
A terrible price to pay.

Onlookers will never forget
As Rami clutched to his dad,
The atmosphere was horrific,
Shocked the nation and made them feel sad.

Fatally struck in the stomach,
With one final groan Rami fell,
After all the screaming and shouting,
His dad was unconscious as well.

Triggered by the visit of Sharon,
To Islam's holiest shrine,
Israeli opposition leader,
Thinking everything would be fine.

Palestinians will cease their fire,
Eighteen are already dead.
Rami's dad among the injured,
Is now in a hospital bed.

Rioting in West Bank will stop,
Or so we've all been told,
It's been the worst to hit the Gaza Strip,
For Rami was twelve years old.

Nicole Sugg (14)
Gaynes School

THE BALLAD OF THE KURSK

For the men on board the Kursk
it was their last voyage when
the torpedo blew up the hull of
the ship.

All of the men were vaporised in
a few seconds, the rest of the crew
had no clue, the rest of the fleet
were totally in the blue.

The others aboard the Kursk
got flung against steel walls
and were instantly killed
by the impact.

Within twenty minutes all
of the crew were killed
no one had a chance to
even raise an alarm.

Nearby a US sub
heard all on its
sonar and raised the
alarm at last.

The Russians tried a
cover-up and said they
were still alive, little
did the people know!

But soon they found out
that the sailors
were all
long-gone.

William Simpson (13)
Gaynes School

KILLED BY 118 BODY PIERCINGS

The tattoo arts of piercing body parts,
Body rings and belly bars
More metal than in cars
Never to be seen again, now we all sit in pain

Lesley was only young
Her story now makes people glum
Her hygiene was poor
Now only in our hearts for evermore

Doctors were never her thing
Not for a pain or not for a sting
She never thought she would become ill
She fell into a coma, now we suffer the deal

Septicaemia and a heart attack
Hepatitis C and her hygiene lack
Llanelle, South Wales with an unknown date
She was the one, she was God's bait

Doomed on Millennium Eve
A hobby that makes some people heave
Jerry Springer shows were the life for her
Then when she collapsed that evening
                    it all became a blur.

Rachel Coppen (13)
Gaynes School

THE SEA

The sea is a growling leopard
staring at the cliffs
swaying back and forth

Groaning at the passers-by
turning their heads
to an awesome cry

Her white whiskers spray
our faces
telling us to keep away

The smell of her breath
attracted you to
this lonely place.

Michelle Gilby (14)
Gaynes School

THE MAGNIFICENT GEORGIAN

The war was over,
An iron curtain descends,
Stalin was victorious,
Communism had won its friends

Germany paid for the Fuhrer's crimes,
Their curtain was rapidly drawn,
Stalin had become a hero,
And a new legacy was born.

Half of the world was in the red,
Stalin wanted not the half, but the whole,
In old age he dreamt eagerly,
About his lifelong goal.

The people's dictator was old,
But *he* was the man of steel,
He knew he began to feel weak,
But death wasn't in the deal.

Uncle Joe died a slow death,
On the 5th of March 1953,
Will purges be needed for power?
Or will it be won by decree?

Will Stalin's purges stop?
Will Stalin's crimes relent?
Will Stalin's communism die?
Will Stalin's new leader repent?

The devil had died,
I'll give you one guess,
To those lists of questions
Which caused distress?

Tim Aker (15)
Gaynes School

ENGLISH BALLAD

Princess Diana was as soft as a rose
She filled our lives with so many glows
She brought peace and hope throughout the world.
Her love spread through every boy and girl.

She lived in London with her sons
But now has departed from her little ones
They now have appeared to have moved on
But still remembers all she has done.

Her death came as a complete shock
And time stood still on every clock
Her funeral was a lovely thing
With Elton John there to sing.

Now that three years have passed
We still remember her face at last
For she will always be the Queen of Hearts
Forever and always till death do us part.

Lauren Wilkins (13)
Gaynes School

PAULA YATES

We met in 1994
The birds sang in the trees.
The flowers were all blooming
My life was now at ease

Michael was my saviour
Our Tiger Lily was then born
We were a happy unit
How my life was to be torn.

Why did you go and leave me?
You didn't even say.
We didn't even say goodbye
It was a sad, lonely day.

I couldn't cope without your love
The drink and drugs took over
The world around me fell apart
My memories were in clover.

But now we are together,
We two will be as one
Just like the day we fell in love
Our two lives are now one.

'Wake up, Mummy,' Tiger said.
The sky was blue, birds singing too.
'Wake up Mummy,' Tiger said
She did not know her mum was dead.

> *On a tragic September day,*
> *Paula Yates took her life away.*

Sasha White (13)
Gaynes School

THE BALLAD OF DUNBLANE

It was March in 1996
As the children went to school,
The sky was grey and cloudy
And the wind was very cool.

It seemed like just another day
The classroom looked the same,
And all seemed quite familiar
In the little school of Dunblane.

One man felt outside it all
Who hid his life in sadness,
Who wanted to be liked and known
But slipped away to madness.

Filled with rage and crazy thoughts
He heard their sounds of cheer,
The happy sounds of fun and songs
Turned to cries of fear,

As the madman burst into school
The massacre began,
The shooting of a gun was loud,
Children grabbed the teacher's hand.

Sixteen children died that day
He took a teacher's life,
He turned the gun upon himself
Now he has paid the price.

The parents of the children mourn
Because the man was insane,
Will the town ever be the same
Without the children of Dunblane?

Natalie Frost (14)
Gaynes School

Diana's Death

Was she the 'People's Princess'?
It was a tragedy when she died
People were in a lot of stress
They remembered when she was
                    a beautiful bride.

A fateful night in Paris
In a car with Dodi Fayed
The driver, he was harassed
And in the crash they both died.

The country went into mourning
Her sons in private cried
And as daybreak was dawning
They couldn't believe she had died.

Was she the 'People's Princess'?
It was a tragedy when she died
Was she just a model in fancy dress
Or just the Prince's bride?

Elizabeth Bamford (14)
Gaynes School

PRINCESS DIANA
1961-1997

Diana was a lovely, young girl,
Who was known all over the world,
She was loved for her heart and generosity,
Like a new baby waiting to be held.

Diana put on a very brave face
Which everyone else could see,
You could blame the press for Diana's death,
All she wanted was to be free.

When she and Charles got married
It was a wonderful day,
Although she enjoyed every minute of it
The press still got in their way.

Privacy was something that Diana never had
Even when she had her two sons,
Although the press were always there
Diana still tried to have fun.

At the end of a disappointing marriage
Diana's lifestyle changed,
She started supporting more charities
As caring was Diana's main aim.

When she fell in love with Dodi,
The press were always there
With an attempt to get away from it
Sadly, this ended their tragic affair.

Diana was killed in a car crash,
With Dodi by her side,
Many hearts were broken by this news

Diana, you shouldn't have died!

Natalie Sharp (13)
Gaynes School

FORMULA 1

The start of the race in Formula 1
The one that Michael Schumacher won.
The drivers were going faster and faster
But did not know that there would be a disaster.

The disaster started on the first corner
As their tyres were ready to burn
A tyre flew up ready to kill
As a marshall died from a flying wheel.

The race carried on after the bash
People were shocked after the crash
Drivers were scared to go fast
In the back of their mind was the blast

People were worried about Formula 1
After the incident that had been done
Fans still turned up to the next race
The cars still drove at an enormous pace.

Ricky Webb (14)
Gaynes School

SARAH PAYNE

Where is Sarah, Mother?
Where has Sarah gone?
Is there something wrong, Mother,
Because you're normally very strong?

I can feel your pain
I can see it in your eyes
When you turn and look at me,
I feel it's all just lies.

Sarah has been missing now
For what seems very long
I wish she was right here with me
So we could sing our little song.

Minutes, hours, days have passed
But we have heard nothing to last
To give us hope, joy and glory
I wish that this was not my story.

The time has come for us to change
Our family, not as one
For we are missing part of it
Sarah Payne, our beloved one.

She was a sister to be proud of
Who had a cheerful smile
To hear her voice is something
That makes life worthwhile.

She was a sister who brought happiness
To her family every day
For she warmed so many moments
With her thoughtful, loving way.

I hope you're looking down on me now?

Stacey Martin (13)
Gaynes School

STEPHEN LAWRENCE BALLAD

He was a normal person like you and me,
Except that he was black,
But some thugs saw him as unusual,
They decided to cut him some slack.

Whilst waiting at the bus stop one night,
For a bus to take him home,
Some white people came and jumped him,
He was hopeless and alone.

His parents sat and waited for him,
But still he did not come.
They were yet to know of the tragedy,
That death had come to their son.

So now they say goodbye to their son,
The boy they loved the best,
Now he is safe up there in Heaven,
Now he can lie down to rest.

James Driver (13)
Gaynes School

HILLSBOROUGH DISASTER

Where's Daddy, Mummy?
When is he coming home?
I have to ask Daddy the score, Mummy.
I wonder if Liverpool won?

It has been four hours, Mummy,
And Daddy is still not home,
He might have been beaten up, Mummy,
Try him on his phone.

Who's on the phone, Mummy?
Is it Dad on the 'dog and bone'?
Why are you crying, Mummy?
It's only Dad on the phone.

It's been twenty-four hours, Mummy,
And Daddy is still not home,
I'm getting worried, Mummy,
Because Daddy may not be coming home.

Dad's on the TV, Mummy,
He looks like he is in pain,
They said it happened yesterday, Mummy.
They said it's a real shame.

Now you tell me, Mummy,
He will not be coming home,
You said he got crushed, Mummy,
And now we are all alone.

Gary Reeder (13)
Gaynes School

THE BOMBING OF MI6

It was the night of September
When MI6 lost its members
In the bombing of the night
Which we all remember.

>The night was quiet
>All was quiet
>Nothing happened
>Nothing was harmed.

Suddenly the sky lit up
All was alerted
Was it a bird, a plane?
No, it was a missile that came.

>There was a crash
>And a flash like lightning
>The police ran over fast
>To find themselves fighting

They had to fight their minds
Had to believe what happened
Why did they do it?
Why did it happen?

>The news was broadcast
>On radio and television
>They told the public,
>It caused such confusion.

Matthew Skingsley (13)
Gaynes School

MY BALLAD FOR PERFORMANCE

It was the Final of the European Cup,
Manchester United v Bayern Munich.
Fans had gathered to see the game,
But which team would get the fame?

Bayern Munich were the first to score,
A free kick by Mario Barlar in the sixth minute.
Manchester United's heads went down,
Alex Ferguson wore a frown.

Manchester United were battling hard, but not hard enough,
Because Bayern hit the bar and post.
'Whistle', it was half-time at the Nou Camp,
And it was raining hard, making the pitch very damp.

'Whistle', the second half began,
Who knew who would win?
A disallowed goal for United,
But this didn't matter because they kept on fighting.

There were three minutes left,
It was still 1-0,
David Beckham took a kick,
Sheringham had a shot, it had to hit!

Goal! It was 1-1,
They had got the draw but could they win?
David Beckham had another kick,
Could they score? Goal! They had done it!

Glenn Salmon (13)
Gaynes School

TITANIC

The Titanic was a grand ship,
just the place for families,
who wanted to travel to America,
and the only way was overseas.

The engines were pushed to go faster,
so they would get there a day early,
their speed would be on the news that night,
for everybody to see.

But ahead lay an iceberg,
that they had spotted too late,
water began to fill the ship,
and all their loved ones could do was wait.

There weren't enough lifeboats on board,
especially for third-class men,
people were fighting for their lives,
but the boats were for children and women.

All you could hear was screaming,
as the ship was pulled under,
all the people felt the shooting pain,
from the shock of the ice-cold water.

Thousands of dead bodies were floating,
and people knew there was death ahead,
Titanic did make the news that night,
but the headline was different,
it was thousand people dead!

The help had come much too late,
but when it finally did come,
guess how many boats had come back for them?
It's unbelievable, just one.

A lot of people still think of Titanic today,
and most people shed a tear,
but only the people that were on the ship
can understand the true fear.

Husniye Kabay (13)
Gaynes School

SMILING

Smiling is infectious,
You can catch it like the flu.
When someone smiled at me today,
I started smiling too.

I passed it round the corner,
And someone saw me grin.
And when he smiled, I realised,
I'd passed it on to him.

It don't take much time to smile.
It really is quite easy.
Don't groan or frown or be unhappy,
So come along, get cheesy.

Be nice and pass a smile,
To everyone you see,
And let it pass around the world,
And let it include me.

It only costs seventeen muscles,
All around your face,
Start smiling now and spread it all,
Around the human race.

Though you're having an argument,
You should smile every day,
It doesn't matter if you've got no teeth,
Just smile anyway.

So if you see a smile begin,
Don't leave it undetected,
Let's start a chain around the world,
And get the globe infected.

Stacey Plumb (12)
Gaynes School

THE INTERNET

The Internet, it is always alive,
Finding web pages on cookies and spies
People in chat rooms, talking about cars,
People looking and reading about stars.

Dot Com this and Dot Com that,
Do Co Dot UK, Dot Org and all that.
Web pages on ringing tones,
Web pages on ice-cream cones.
Web pages on army careers,
Web pages on all kinds of beers.
All this and more can be found on the Internet,
But try not to spend all your time on it,
And get yourself into debt.

Daniel Yates (12)
Gaynes School

THE COMPUTER

Technical computer sitting silent.

Suddenly lights start flashing vigorously,
CD drives revving noisily.
The computer comes alive,
And takes you for a ride.

Through wires and plugs,
Faster than light,
Not knowing if it's day,
Or if it's night.

You fire at tanks on video games,
You blow up their bases, and shoot in their faces.
You surf on the web,
Searching for cars to shoot to the stars.

You enter disks with dazzling colours,
Like the rainbow spectrum, in your glasses' reflection.
Suddenly the lights stop flashing vigorously,
CD drives stop revving noisily.

The computer starts to wind down, it stops,
There's no sound!

Technical computer sitting silently . . .

Joe Townshend (13)
Gaynes School

WORLD WAR II

The smell of burning and thick, black smoke.
Day turns to night, nothing can be seen.
The injured lie dying on the ground.
They cannot make a sound, except to choke.

The sound of guns firing fills the air.
Tanks rumble slowly past.
Planes overhead dive swiftly
A piercing scream. War is unfair.

The silence that follows will not last.
The soldiers rest and patch up their wounds.
Reloading their guns. Preparing for another attack

Which will happen as it has done in the past.

Jedd Barry (12)
Gaynes School

COMPUTERS

Grey PlayStation being played daily,
Small memory card saving slowly.
Dual-shock controller vibrating solidly.
Super Dodge Viper racing quickly,
Around the cool race track.

Tiny Dreamcast working silently,
White VMS saving and being played.
Weird controller, big and chunky.
Philippoussis blasting the ball,
Bashing it around the tennis court.

Black N64 playing cartridges,
Little memory card in the controller.
Big controller with an analogue stick.
Moustached Mario in a castle,
Rescuing a princess called Peach.

Mini Colour Game Boy that's very small,
It has a massive memory card.
It comes in multiple colours.
You are Ash, a boy from Pallet,
You have to collect Pokémon.

All these computers are very cool,
Everybody should own one.
If you don't you're very weird,
And you will have no fun!

Joe Honer (12)
Gaynes School

NOTHING'S WORSE THAN BEING BORED

Nothing's worse than being bored,
Those rainy days I hate.
Maybe one day laws will be passed,
That boredom will just have to wait,
Boredom will just have to take an unofficial hike,
And also I think boredom should be banned from human sight.

If boredom were to go on trial,
I would go a certain mile,
To make sure that boredom got,
Lined up against a wall and shot.
If boredom got the chop instead,
I could mount its ugly head
Upon my empty bedroom wall:
Or maybe it could hang instead outside my door,
Or should it go beneath my bed?

Maybe I could launch a petition,
Or it might just be my own soul's mission
To remove this thing call boredom,
Maybe I could buy a vacuum,
And suck this problem out of sight.

As I come to the end of this,
What is my boredom analysis?
There is something you must learn,
That is if you feel concern
That boredom is just one short turn
From coming in and taking over,
Please feel free to drop this boredom,
Off the big white cliffs of Dover.

David Makepeace (12)
Gaynes School

MY DAD

A nything I want, I ask my dad
B ecause he is the kindest man I know.
C omforts me when I'm sad
D oesn't let his anger show
E xpects me to do well in school
F amily is his main concern
G oes to watch me play football
H elps me with things I need to learn
I n the summer caravan we go
J et-skiing and boating are lots of fun.
K eeping him busy, he has grass to mow
L ies down on the beach in the baking sun
M akes me laugh sometimes, my dad
N o one treats me like he does
O ften when he is sad
P oems for him make him glad
Q uiet I have to be when he is sleeping
R owdy I am when he's not
S noring loudly, awake we are keeping
T ime for us to moan a lot
U nderstanding is my dad
V ery busy like a bumblebee
W ants his family to have it all
X XL not small
Y ou now know about my dad
Z ippedy-do-dah, *I love my dad.*

Gemma Horner (12)
Gaynes School

CRAZINESS

Be not feared, so withered, dried-up like a sultana,
In that corner day and night wondering when he would be shed,
He sunk backwards with his shelly shade of pain,
His heartbeat grew faster as his colour changed a shade of red,
He pondered as he was, a man dressed in white,
He wondered what he would say to himself that night,
Thinking of his family, I wonder,
Once more the eye of terrible aspects,
Wondering if he was going to die or stay alive,
For what care have I got for words but words do so well,
I hear her speak yet I say nothing,
I hear her tiptoe in my mind.

Bianca Felton (12)
Gaynes School

TECHNOLOGY IN THE 21ST CENTURY

Cool games' console entertaining the world
Fast computers living lives of their own
Confusing video recorder getting harder to programme
Digital stereos sounding even better
Slimming televisions getting smaller.

3D cinemas zapping our brains.
Entertaining DVD players storing more information.
Speedy microwaves cooking for the world.
Chilly fans cooling the house.
Dynamic speakers shrinking down in size.

Intelligent mobile phones surfing the Net.
Digital watches taking pictures.
Surround sound becoming more 3D
Vacuum cleaners cleaning towards dual-cyclone.
Hot irons uncreasing our clothes.

Space-wasting fax machines shrinking in size.
Flashing disco lights confusing our brains
Portable audio getting smaller and smaller and smaller.

Mirran Carpenter (12)
Gaynes School

THE OLYMPIC ATHLETE

Four years of hard training,
Four years of keeping fit,
Must never lose the confidence,
Must have the strength and power to win.

Must not lose your bottle
Against the experienced athlete,
Must just think of your ability,
Believe in yourself.

The race is about to start,
Do you have the guts to win?
Build the confidence for the final race,
And, on the blocks and *go!*

I'm in 3rd place and looking good,
But I'm back into 4th place, bad news,
Must keep confidence, and
I'm back in 3rd place.

Halfway, I've got some energy left,
I've had it, I'm going for gold,
I'm in 2nd, and now joint 1st,
5 metres left, first touch wins and *I've won!*

I can't believe it, I'm the Olympic Champion,
My country is cheering,
I'm on the podium, I've got gold,
My effort paid off, *I'm the Olympic Champ.*

Scott Denham (12)
Gaynes School

CANOPY

In the deep and the dark
and the thickness of the jungle
where the vines and plants and leeches suck your blood.

In the night there's a roar
as you start to run but stumble
the roar ever growing closer
there's no time to stop and wonder what it is.

Poison darts, sound of feet
of the tribesman and the hunters
that go creeping through the bushes patiently.

Greedy raiders of the tombs
of the ancient civilisations
That leave behind their temples and the sacrifices brutal in their land.

By the swamp there's a bank
on which piles of skulls and bones are lying
waiting for their murd'rers to return.

What is this? Chasm deep
with a rope bridge swaying rapidly
a plank falls down for what seems like an hour.

As you roam lost but calm
as you heartbeat's growing faster
and you're speeding up your paces but for what?

You stumble on a shrine
An oracle to jungle spirits, and there it is
your desire, the Emerald of Eternal Life.

You reach out your shaking hand
but from the gem come screams of anger
you feel your soul is draining from your mind.

Then you're gone; now one of us,
the protectors of the Emerald,
With a scream
that rings
throughout
the canopy . . .

Molly White (12)
Gaynes School

SOLOMON

Through the darkness of the mist
Lies a long and daunting list.
Pictures and words fill my mind,
Of the world we left behind.

Anger, suffering, hatred and pain.
Pictures of men crying in vain.
Children screaming
And angels dreaming.

A sword and a shield.
A man in a field.
Not fighting
Just writing.

He feels the heat of the sun beaming down.
Whilst listening to music coming from town.
When all of a sudden he puts down his pen
And screams out loud 'My son, Solomon!'

Rachel Harriett (12)
Gaynes School

TORTURED BY MY DREAM

The leaves did rustle upon the ground,
From the door came a crackling sound.
Inside the hall the cobwebs hung,
And from the corner the bats swung.
A draught whistled around my feet,
When I heard footsteps like a drumming beat.

I ran as fast as my feet could bear,
When I tripped and fell into a vampire's lair.
The blood-fleshed smell sent me a-shiver,
The skulls on the floor made me quiver.
I began to scream but no sound came out,
I tried and tried but I couldn't shout.
I found myself shaking in my bed,
Was it a dream or all in my head?

The doctors came to take me away,
An injection for some peace is what I pray.
These dark, ugly thoughts will never go,
They come to scare me when I'm feeling low.

Lucy Vickress (12)
Gaynes School

GRANDAD

I loved my grandad and I still do.

He was like my bodyguard,
I slept on his belly.
He knew nearly everything,
Because of the telly.

I loved my grandad and I still do.

It's been five whole years,
Since he's been gone.
I cried nearly all night long.

I loved my grandad and I still do.

His hair was silver,
His heart was gold.
Around my body
His arms would fold.

I loved my grandad and I still do.

I would've loved,
To keep him forever.
But I'm afraid
That would happen never.

I loved my grandad and I still do.

His clear, square glasses,
Were so sweet.
He would spoil us,
With lots of treats.

I loved my grandad and I still do.

He was as loving,
As could be.
He meant the world
To me.

Georgina O'Hanlon (12)
Gaynes School

HORSES

They gallop along, ever so fast,
They stop and chew on the long, green grass.
Horses, they have no need to worry,
No need to rush and no need to hurry.
Their long bristly tails sway side to side,
They sway even more when you go for a ride.
They walk, trot and canter whenever you say,
Horses have such a wonderful way.
They come in all sizes, colours and shapes,
They really can be a person's best mate.
They jump over the jumps like a spring,
Horses really are beautiful things.
They gobble down their oats and then lie in the hay,
Ready for an action-packed day.

They wake up bright and early ready for a saddle on their back,
All set for a race on the long, winding track.
The gun bangs and the horses make a run,
The day at the races is really fun.
Fifty feet left of the race,
Who is going to win first place?
Tall shiny trophies, colourful rosettes,
Who is going to win the bet?

The races end and the horse goes to rest,
The jockey feels he has done his best.
It's time to muck out, with a fork and a broom,
Then it's time for the horse to be groomed.
So many brushes, which one shall I use?
First I will clean the horse's hooves,
Lock the stable, push each bolt into place,
Let the horse rest, ready for another race.

Bobbie Brandon (12)
Gaynes School

THE MAN IN THE MOON

The man in the moon
Always smiles at you
Through happiness and despair
So when you're down
Don't put on a frown
Just look up in the air.

Genevieve Beard (11)
Hassenbrook GM School

THE JUMPER

I hate jumpers more every day
the way they itch and itch all the time,
they never stop and won't give up.

Gary Bonning (11)
Hassenbrook GM School

TICK-TOCK

Tick-tock goes the clock on the wall.
Its sharp hands go round pointing to the numbers
Its perfect round face is still as a mouse.
The clock looks unhappy.

Tick-tock goes the clock on the wall.
The broken cuckoo comes out not moving
Or talking at all.

Tick-tock goes the clock on the wall.

Aimee Johnson (11)
Hassenbrook GM School

THE SNAIL

The snail slid
slowly over the garden,
leaving a silvery trail.
He spotted a bird, and hid
away until that bird
stole him away.

Kayleigh North (11)
Hassenbrook GM School

A TYPICAL PLANE

The massive wheels, the roaring engine,
The porthole windows,
A smooth landing,
Paradise views,
The tightly-dressed hostesses,
Terrified passengers,
A typical plane.

Jack Conway (11)
Hassenbrook GM School

GRANDAD'S DENTURES

They snap, they bite!
They come out at night
The fantastic adventures
Of Grandad's dentures

They snap, they bite!
They've vanished from sight
(But where have they gone?
You'll know later on.)
The fantastic adventures
Of Grandad's dentures

They snap, they bite!
Grandad fought them one night
They were under the table
With a sticky label
These were the adventures
Of Grandad's dentures!

Kieran Flanagan (12)
Hassenbrook GM School

TIME

Tick-tock, tick-tock, time is ticking away,
Very soon time has passed and taken another day.
As time goes by we all grow very, very old,
A lot of precious time is wasted but we will not be told.
Day by day, month by month and even year by year,
We all share laughs, we all share smiles and we all shed a tear.
Some people worry about the future and worry about what they
will say,
But so far in my experience I've learnt to live for today.
Don't waste time on worrying about tomorrow because tomorrow is
never here,
Achieve your goals today and enjoy the quality time every minute of
the year.

Hollie Pell (12)
Hassenbrook GM School

POOR OLD FRED

There once was a tortoise named Fred
Who loved the herbaceous bed
He munched all day long
Whilst singing a song
He grew so fat
His shell eventually went splat!

Kirsty Moisley (12)
Hassenbrook GM School

HASSENBROOK TEACHERS

There was an old lady, Mrs Burt,
Who was a great big flirt,
She goes to the clubs
And some discos and pubs,
Does the flirty old lady, Mrs Burt.

There was a lady, Mrs O'Leary
Who always had a big query,
She's really cool
And she works in our school,
Does that lady called Mrs O'Leary.

There was a young lady, Miss Yates
Who likes to go on dates,
She's really, really funny
And has got a fair bit of money,
Has our history teacher, Miss Yates.

There is a young lady, Miss Kay
Who teaches PE every day,
She runs up and down
And she never does frown,
Does the PE teacher, Miss Kay.

Sarah Owen (12)
Hassenbrook GM School

SECRET ADMIRER

I look at you and see your beauty,
I watch you walking right near me
Your hair is messy but I'm not bothered,
Cos I'm your secret admirer.

I watch you talking, I feel your lips,
Smooth upon my cheek,
I need you now, please notice me,
Cos I'm your secret admirer.

I often dream about you,
Your kind and thoughtful ways,
I'm sad when you're not here,
The day just seems so dull
I need you now, I really do,

Cos I'm your secret admirer.

Joanna Pemberton (12)
Hassenbrook GM School

THE OLD MAN FROM KENT

There was an old man from Kent
Who liked to visit Trent
He liked it so much
He bought his own hutch
Up there in Stoke-On-Trent.

Natalie Godward (12)
Hassenbrook GM School

YOU

You were always there,
Sometimes when you weren't wanted.
I put up with it,
But often told you to go away.
What was the point of us carrying on?
The answer is,
There wasn't one.
We gave up but you wouldn't let go.
You got depressed,
I got worried.
We got back together,
And it started all over again.
The pain,
The sorrow.
I got fed up.
We were through for good.
Now I must forget,
And see through you when you get depressed.
Face it.
It's over.
We're through.

Katie Vear (12)
Hassenbrook GM School

TEACHER AND CHILD

Mrs Nicol's young child name Frances,
Does ever such beautiful dances
She's as pretty as flowers,
She dances for hours
Does Mrs Nicol's young child named Frances.

There was a young lady, Mrs Nicol
Who was in a great big pickle
She doesn't know why but neither do I
She's in a big pickle, Mrs Nicol.

There was a young lady Mrs Cattini
When on holiday she wears a bikini
She is really pretty
And ever so witty
Is that lovely young lady, Mrs Cattini.

There was a young lady, Mrs Towell,
Who is a new maths teacher now
She has a good skill
And is really brill
So our new maths teacher, Mrs Towell.

Emily Hull (12)
Hassenbrook GM School

WITHOUT YOU

Without you
I would be so lonely
My heart would be an empty ship
Sailing on a deserted sea.

Without you
The fun we used to have
Would be history
The games we played
Would be torn from my
            broken heart.

Matthew Holding (12)
Hassenbrook GM School

MY NEW TEACHER

My new teacher has a booming voice that
Roars like a lawnmower cutting grass.

My new teacher stands over me like the
Massive tree in my back garden.

My new teacher is as friendly as a
Hungry pussy cat, or so he says!

My new teacher tries to be funny as
Funny as a clown in the circus.

My new teacher is very clever as clever
As the champion of 'Mastermind.'

My new teacher arrives every day,
Looking as smart as fresh paint.

My new teacher seems very nice
As nice as a home baked apple pie.

Joe Wilson (12)
Hassenbrook GM School

MY NEW TEACHER

My new teacher's a crafty cat,
But he wouldn't let anyone tell him that,
He is as smart as a penguin on a dinner date,
But he would never dream of being late.

He's as precise as the movement on a clock,
The school day passes . . . tick . . . tock,
He's as loud as a foghorn on a boat
And all this noise comes from his throat,
A scary ghost story on a winter's night,
The amount of homework will give you a fright.

But apart from that he is really quite fun,
It's my new teacher Mr . . .

Joanne Myler (12)
Hassenbrook GM School

MY NEW TEACHER

My new teacher is . . .

As pretty as a swan drifting quietly across the water,
Her job as a teacher earns her much more than a quarter,
She's as nice as a roast dinner on a Sunday,
I can't wait to see her in school on Monday.

She's as smart as a woman dressed for an interview,
I really like her I bet you would too,
She's as funny as a comedian on a TV show,
She's as quiet as a mouse oh wouldn't you know.

Well that is it about my new teacher,
If you're as nice as her I can't wait to meet ya!

Billie Baker (12)
Hassenbrook GM School

MY NEW TEACHER

My new teacher is loud like a choir in a concert,
Beautiful blonde hair like Goldilocks.
Thin like a wafer,
Tidy like a cleaner,
Helpful like clues of a detective story,
Smart the same as an answer book.
She is as kind as a lady handing out sweets,
Caring like a hospital.

Jenna Hall (11)
Hassenbrook GM School

RAINY DAYS

It's a rainy day,
Inside we have to stay,
There is falling rain,
I am going insane,
The clouds look glum and dark,
I can't go to the park,
I can't go out to play
It's such a boring day.

Louise Woodcock (11)
Hassenbrook GM School

MY DUCK MAISY

My duck Maisy,
Drives us really, really crazy.
When you think of a
Duck's life, it's rather lazy.

She's up at the crack of dawn,
Quacking to get out on the lawn.
She flip flaps round the garden
Looking for a little morsel or a bargain.

She loves mum's fuschias and hosters,
Which she will eat pots and pots of.
Luckily the geraniums are up high,
Mind you I suppose she could always fly.

Lettie Nice (11)
Hassenbrook GM School

APRIL FOOL!

A toad in the sink while I'm having a wash,
Ha, ha, very funny Josh.

Swimming instructor there's a shark in the pool,
Now we'll see who's an April Fool!

I got Billy Bunten with a squirting flower,
Eleven o'clock, just one more hour.

A worm in your pasta, there's no way of proving,
Teacher this one seems to be moving.

12 o'clock, lunch time, the ticking ends here,
No more 'Tom Foolery' until next year.

Jordan Gray (11)
Hassenbrook GM School

My New Teacher

My new teacher,
Is as forgetful as an elephant,
She's always losing her glasses.

My new teacher,
Is as funny as a clown,
She's always trying to make us laugh.

My new teacher,
Likes to be different,
She's as different as the two colours
Black and white.

My new teacher,
Is quite neat,
She's as neat as somebody in a
Handwriting competition.

My new teacher,
Is very kind,
She's as kind as a charity worker.

My new teacher,
Is all these things,
Which makes her really friendly.

I like my new teacher.

Rebecca Goldsmith (11)
Hassenbrook GM School

MY NEW TEACHER

As accurate as a homing missile
what a good description
of a teacher I know
do carry on and listen.

Still water can be calm
as is this teacher I know
he's as clever as a computer
nowhere near as slow.

My new teacher and James Bond
both dress very smart
both are tall as trees
it's hard to tell them apart.

Dennis Bergkamp plays for Arsenal
a great player of the ball
my teacher does not dribble
but at cutting and sawing, he's skilful.

A comedian is funny
a judge is very fair
my teacher is both of these
that's why I like it when I'm there.

Ian Mackenzie (11)
Hassenbrook GM School

MY NEW TEACHER

Teachers are like species,
All of them are different
And on my second day at Hassenbrook
I met another new teacher.
This teacher is certainly not dull
Because her middle name is Cheery
She never seems sad or unhappy
She's fun like a puppy wanting to play
Unhelpful teachers give a bad impression
My teacher is helpful like a good friend
It would be very odd if she wasn't clever
But she's a clever clogs brimming with knowledge,
She's cool headed and calm
She doesn't panic or get flustered,
She's smart like a new pin,
She's definitely not untidy,
She's talkative like a budgie,
Not afraid to raise her voice,
If you said she was tall, you'd be wrong,
She's small like a mouse,
My teacher is blonde and bubbly
She has glasses that she wears sometimes,
Her subject is maths
And her name is . . .

Mrs . . .

Chloe Flame (11)
Hassenbrook GM School

MY NEW TEACHER

My new teacher has a bellowing voice,
It's like the bang of a bomb!
But yet he's ever so friendly
And as funny as a clown!

My new teacher is as tall as a giraffe
And as firm as a brick wall!
He's as plump as a cushion
And his beard is as bristly as a bear's fur!

Now I bet you want to know,
Who my new teacher is.
I've given you all these clues,
. . . is who my new teacher is!

Hannah Southgate (11)
Hassenbrook GM School

MY NEW TEACHER

A friendly smile,
A caring face.

She's average height
And average size
And she always has
A twinkle in her eyes.

She loses this and loses that
And she thinks she's as blind as a bat.

She's as wise as an owl
With the language she speaks
And as bright as a button,
In the subject she teaches.

She's as happy as a lark
And as bright as a spark
And has eyes in the back of her head,
I'm told.

She has a heart of gold,
Which nobody could steal,
But is also very strict,
I feel.

A friendly smile,
A caring face,
It will take a lot to keep up with her pace.

Victoria Elise King (12)
Hassenbrook GM School

My New Teacher

We have a new teacher in our class
The old one was fed up.

He has . . . a menacing smile
Which makes him a devil,
Ears that could hear a hatching chick
A mile away.
He makes kids not want to come back
The following day.
He's got a thunderous voice
That echoes through the school.
He's as cunning as a fox with
Eyes that survey everything
Like a falcon.
Can you guess? It's Mr . . .

Shaun McIntosh (12)
Hassenbrook GM School

MY NEW TEACHER

My new teacher will certainly beat ya,
In his subject PE.
He's very athletic, to him I'm pathetic,
That's why he's so nice to me.

He teaches us lots of skills,
But although they sometimes kill,
They are lots and lots of fun.

He's completely proud but ever so loud
And his shout can be heard from miles around,
He's supportive and informative,
All knowledge is his.

By now you should have guessed,
Who my new teacher is.

Yes, it's Mr . . .

Adam Bulpitt (11)
Hassenbrook GM School

IN MY HEAD

I   think a lot
N ow there's a thought

M aybe I'll stay in bed today,
Y es I think I will.

H ow I wonder what would happen, if I slept till noon,
E veryone is laughing as I daydream on
A nd still I stand out in the street watching them go by,
D own, down into my thoughts I go.

Thomas Robinson (11)
Hassenbrook GM School

MILLENNIUM PARTY

Everyone dancing merrily,
Adults thinking of wine before thinking of tea
Sausage rolls laying on the table,
When people have finished drinking, they'll dance, if they're able
Children staying clear of the bar,
They think dancing, like loonies, is better by far
There's barely any adults left sober,
Yet the party's nowhere near over,
Look! It's finally midnight,
Some people raise their glasses, some jump up and down, what a sight.
At one o'clock children are so tired they drag their feet and
                                    droop their heads,
As granny sends them off to bed.

Hannah Shilling (11)
Hassenbrook GM School

My New Teacher

My new teacher is as loud as a foghorn
This teacher is built like a tank
As strict as a sergeant major
And as fit as a fiddle.

My new teacher has a heart of a lion
He is like continuous alarm clock's ringing,
This teacher has the guts of ten men
He seems to be as big as the Titanic when you're next to him.

My new teacher is as strong as an ox
And has the courage of a lion
This teacher won't give up easily
My new teacher can make you feel as tiny as a mouse.

My new teacher is as broad as a bulldozer
This teacher is not agile like a ballerina
This teacher has nerves of steel
My teacher is . . .

Gary Shilling (11)
Hassenbrook GM School

DREAMZ

You dream while you sleep
Without a peep
A snore, a sound, a thing,
But if you like sleeping,
Then you will start dreaming
Without a sound or a peep.
Then I will sleep, sleep.

Danny Chippendale (12)
New Rush Hall School

I Miss

I miss my family,
I miss my home,
I miss watching TV,
I miss using the phone.

I miss my bed,
I miss my videos,
I miss my name always being said,
I miss being bad then being told.

Stuart Edwards (13)
New Rush Hall School

BOXES

Boxes are transparent,
All around you,
Over.
Under.
Either side.

Boxes are the things that
Make us feel a
Success
Or
Failure.

Boxes are in our mind,
Containing our
Thoughts
Dreams
Reality.

Boxes are the restraints
Of religion
Money
Work
And play.

Without boxes
We could
Fly
Our minds
The sky
Forever.

Naomi de Berker (17)
Seven Kings High School

DREAMING

When I step into the magnolia room
There's a bucket of paint, a sponge and a broom.
What shall I paint for my dream today
Shall I be in a Shakespearean play?

I'll sit beside a sparkling stream,
With my popular modelling team.
Will I look like Britney Spears?
Even though it will end in tears.

Will I be surrounded by gorgeous boys?
Or, will I be fixing children's toys?
Now it is time to walk back into my room,
But I won't forget to put down the multicoloured broom.

Carley-Anne Miller (12)
Southend High School For Girls

DREAM POEM

I have come to the borders of sleep,
Like the golden gates of heaven, except,
There is no way in.

You struggle but the armed guards, hold you back,
You are pushed down a black hole, except,
The crash never comes.

You are suddenly flying through fluffy white clouds,
Over a calm sea with dolphins splashing, except,
How can you fly with no wings?

You are swimming in the ocean with all the fish,
You listen to the rippling waves above, except,
You are now sitting down on a beach.

There's fire all around you and nails are scraping down blackboards,
There's a horrific scream from behind, except,
You are now wide awake.

Emma Oakley (12)
Southend High School For Girls

MY DREAM

I've come to the borders of sleep,
I've fallen into a hole that's deep,
The colours are bright and calming.
I am flying on a thread of yarn, the
Sound of sweet music is soft to my ears.
I am lifted onto a white deer,
I ride through the forest of a fluttering winter leaf.
I can smell my favourite roast beef!
The deer drops me by a table with one chair, and I sit
Down to eat with a bear, the meat is soft and rare,
Before I know it I am off again, this time on a cloud
The wind whistles through my hair, very loud.
Before I have time to see the sights below me,
I start to fall into that hole again.
It starts to rain but by and by, I wake up
In my warm snugly bed.

Nina Peters (12)
Southend High School For Girls

THE CHANGING DREAM

I had come to the borders of sleep.
And as I dozed, watching the moonlit sky,
She, smiled at me, as my heartbeat slowed,
My once racing pulse, came to almost a stop
And I was in peace, completely at peace.

The room lightened up all of a sudden
And I felt all warm inside,
The sky was a vibrant yellow
And the blue clouds were high in the sky.
The bright white daisies were shining,
With little green bugs everywhere
And I felt the peace, the peace in the air.

Then a few hours later it seemed,
I had walked into a large dark wood,
Where in front of me had jumped my greatest fear . . .
It was dark blue, and hairy with large eyes and pointed teeth
And though it was my greatest fear, I did not know what it was,
Or that it could harm me,
But I knew I had to run.

I turned around and started to run,
Run was my only thought,
Until that dreadful thing slipped in my mind . . .
Surrender.
It forced out, ran and as I was tired,
That nasty thought was all I had.
And somehow I overcame that thought until . . .

Bump!
I had tripped over a moss-covered log.
My fear came upon me. I had felt its breath upon my skin,
As it was about to end the chase,
Until I woke up.

Kathryn Millman (12)
Southend High School For Girls

DREAMS

As I open the gate to the
Garden of dreams,
All feeling of consciousness disappears
As the gate closes
And a path appears in front of me
And I take a step at a time,
I gaze into the distance I'm
Surrounded by joy,
My favourite things emerge
Before me,
Nothing feels strange
Or out of place,
I even feel
Completely relaxed
All my best memories
Rolled into one,
My friends appear before me
And can't seem to stop talking,
But then all the trees develop faces
And the sky turns black,
The sunshine disappears
And my friends die away,
The ground opens up before me
And a great wind sucks me down,
All the memories fade
And I scream out loud,
But no one can hear me
As I silently cry,
Something is ringing,
A sound in my head,
A calling is making
A hole in my dream.

My mum's face is looming over
Me as my dream is pushed to the back of my mind,
The dream soars away as fast as an eagle
It's out of my mind,
Banished from my thoughts forever
As once again the gate to the garden of dreams is closed.

Lucy Marston (12)
Southend High School For Girls

DREAMS FROM HEAVEN TO HELL

Shadows dance around the room,
The victim's life is at its doom,
I think in my motionless sleep,
What dreams I'm going to dream,
The first day, swam the depths of the sea,
The next day shrunk to a buzzing bee,
The next day, won an Olympic gold medal
And danced triumphantly.
Fire to fire, ashes to ashes,
Horrible, distinctive growls and crashes,
Made me wake with a jump,
Finding the covers wrapped round me.
The first day, the voice of a vampire,
The next day saw a mysterious wizard
Who made me jump out of my skin, like a lizard,
The warming glow of morning light,
Thaws me from the dreams that night,
The vivid visions of the night fade,
With the coming of another day.

Louise Rogers (12)
Southend High School For Girls

SLEEP: THE FORBIDDEN OCEAN

I have come to the borders of sleep,
An ocean no one knows how deep
Until they jump in and submerge
In its milky depths.

On the outside, it's blue and inviting,
Underneath it's black and white,
It can make you rich with dreams of gold,
It can fill you with pain and fright.

When you sleep you are safe from all ills
But you can never escape from the one
That fills the bravest with all fear
The black of a nightmare.

The nightmare that can chase
The bravest to the brink
Of a feared insanity
And swallow up any person in despair.

Siobhan O'Shea (13)
Southend High School For Girls

DEEP SLEEP

I have fallen through the borders of sleep,
Deep sleep, a black velvet sky printed with stars.
Dozing, drifting then bang!
The howling wind blew my door shut,
I was in darkness, the light had been blown
Out like a candle.
I can hear screams, shrilling cries for help,
I'm being chased, but I can't run,
I'm falling, faster and faster.
It's getting darker and darker.
I'm falling through space,
A galaxy of planets and stars.
Where I know nothing about what or where I am.
Even who I am.
Only to be found when I awake.

Sophie Moffat (12)
Southend High School For Girls

THE TRICKS OF LIFE

The tricks of life are dreams to me,
For dreams are fantasies, wishes and happy thoughts,
They make people happy, comforted and feel at ease,
People wonder and that's what makes them dream.
Dreams play a huge role in everyone's lives,
For without dreams our nights would seldom
Be looked forward to and the fulfilment
Of life would not be gained.
The light would be destroyed and the
Darkness would triumph.

People dream about things of wealth, love,
Happiness and much more,
Many people become absorbed in dreams
And their dreams feel real,
Until they awaken and realise that
They were fantasising,
Many of us do not realise this
And fantasise forever,
To me dreams are precious
And very rarely a waste of time.

In the years that I have lived,
I have learnt that dreams are tricks
And I will remember this,
Yet I cannot help dreaming dreams,
In a way I feel I am a hypocrite,
For I dream dreams and yet
I believe they do not exist,
Then I look back and rephrase what
I've just thought,
That dreams are tricks of life.

Hareem Sarwar (13)
Southend High School For Girls

I HAD A DREAM

I had a dream
And in my dream I was in a boat,
A boat made of white paper
And in my boat I was drifting across a purple ocean.
Just drifting.
Forwards and backwards.
Rocking to and fro in rhythm with the tide.
To and fro,
To and fro.
Above me was a clear red sky,
No clouds, just sky
And in the sky were stars
And the stars were twinkling.

I had a dream
And in my dream I could hear music,
The music was soft and soothing,
The music made me calm,
As if I was floating.
Just floating.
I was floating in the clear red sky,
I was soaring in and out of the twinkling stars,
In and out,
In and out,
I was soaring through the golden clouds,
I was at peace,
Then I woke up.

Jodie Nel (13)
Southend High School For Girls

MEMORIES OF SLEEP

The thought of my secret dreamland,
Bribes me into leaving reality,
I can hear whistling,
I can feel the water trickling,
Without hesitation, I close the windows to my soul,
In hope of finding a piece of happiness,
That I once knew.

The feeling of floating takes over all,
It was almost motionless,
I can see the sunset fading,
I can feel the warmth on my face,
It is as though I'll never again see,
The world of tears that I belong to,
So much.

Katie Rose (12)
Southend High School For Girls

MY NIGHTMARE POEM

As I come to the borders of sleep,
My mind rests with ease,
I start to dream vividly,
I am on the beach with a dog,
He runs up the cliff side,
I try to get him down but I fail,
I have to go after him,
My foot slips, I gasp and hold on for dear life,
I continue to make my way up,
Up, up, up the cliff side,
The dog is almost there,
I am only halfway,
I am nearly there,
I am out of breath,
My arms and legs are tired,
I feel weak;
I can feel the soft grass at the top,
I take a deep breath and haul myself up,
I think to myself 'I'm there at last!'
Suddenly the cliff gives way,
I fall down, down, down,
Then I am awoken by the sound of my alarm.

Katie Pettitt (12)
Southend High School For Girls

SLEEP

On the borders of sleep
I am waiting, for the dream to grab me,
To pull me in like a vacuum and dust,
I am waiting, to be sucked into a fairy tale
Heaven.

On the borders of sleep,
I am waiting to go,
To a far away place
Where everything is peaceful,
I am waiting to drift like a cloud
In the sky, drift away and fly.

I am on the borders of sleep,
But not quite there, so I wait . . .
I am still waiting and I can see the dream,
Coming quickly flying through the sky,
Like a bird on the wing.

On the borders of sleep I am waiting,
For the dream to grab me
When I am woken,
By the creak of a floorboard,
So the fairy tale dream
Will just have to wait.

Victoria Measom (12)
Southend High School For Girls

DREAMS

I have come to the borders of sleep,
The uncomfortable boundary of being asleep and awake,
When I leave a bustling world, and enter a lonely,
                    deserted area of emptiness.
Like sky on a summer's night
When the cooling air
Rapidly turns from light to dark.
The voices outside
Echo and fade into an unknown blur.
My worries and thoughts diminish
As my eyes begin to close.
New thoughts are created,
Put into an unusual sequence,
Which tells a very strange story.
The sky outside is as black as ebony
But still my sleepy feelings grow,
I fall asleep,
Listening to an imaginary sound of rippling water,
In my mind, vast blue oceans.
I lie asleep, waiting for morning,
So the sky can lighten, and
Once again I can return to reality.

Charlotte Ryan (13)
Southend High School For Girls

THE DREAM

My warm arms, slowly being heated by the sun,
My hair, lightly swaying in the breeze,
My feet, cooling in the trickling stream,
My back, lying gently on the soft green grass,
All is still, peaceful and quiet,
With a smiling face looking out for me,
But when all is still and at its quietest,
The face brings on a glare,
It turns black and small, with green glowing eyes,
Reaching out for me to join him,
In the forest, deep, dark and dull,
The crows slowly circle around my head,
Then whizzing, whizzing, whizzing out of control,
They swoop down and just before they hit,
Ring, ring, I let the phone ring out
As I leave the forest of darkness.

Rebecca Rawle (12)
Southend High School For Girls

I FEAR SHE'S LOST

I am running fast with all my might,
But the lead in my feet,
Is too heavy to bear.

I try so hard, I can't understand
I am getting no further along the road.

I can't stop the rain that's pouring,
Down from my head,
It saturates my body.

I need to reach the screams,
That pierce the cold night air,
I must rescue her.

I fear I will be too late,
If my limbs will not carry me,
I claw myself along.

I can no longer hear,
Those awful screams,
I fear she's lost.

Annie-Jo Poole (12)
Southend High School For Girls

BORDERS OF SLEEP

I have come to the borders of sleep,
I drift like a boat on an emptying lake,
I can hear sounds from streets and houses,
I am half-asleep and half awake.

I'm falling deeper and deeper into sleep,
While dreaming of the day I've left behind
And the day about to dawn,
Oh how I welcome this peaceful state of mind.

I imagine the shouts of laughter
And the agonising cries of pain,
This is too good to be true,
To be sleeping peacefully again.

Alexandra Ross (12)
Southend High School For Girls

TOWN

The town is somewhere you can go,
In sun, rain or snow.
It's a place to relax
And have a load of snacks.
It's a place to see your mate,
It doesn't matter if you're late,
The town is somewhere where you can shop,
It doesn't matter if it's hot.

Justin Young (11)
The James Hornsby High School

My Mum's Pie!

My mum started to make a pie
A scream, a holler and a sigh
She was unable,
To make it stable,
But thought she'd have another try.

Gemma Harris (11)
The James Hornsby High School

THE BARN OWL

The barn owl was in the barn one night,
When the moon was beautiful and bright,
Through its pale misty glow,
The barn owl was seeking gentle snow
Falling from above
And on the floor,
By the old chestnut door,
Sat a little snow white dove.
The owl hooted and flew through the door,
Into the night sky,
Looking around to where the dove did lie.

Kate Elizabeth Freeman (11)
The James Hornsby High School

POSTMAN FRED

There was an old postman called Fred,
Who was scared of a dog called Ted
He took off his shoe
Which was bulky and blue
And slapped Ted around the head.

Alix Fairbrother (11)
The James Hornsby High School

CHEETAH

Its cunning, beady, sneaky eyes,
Vicious, intelligent and very wise.

For who he is, he can't reveal
He's looking for prey and
He's in for the kill.

His creative stare and his nasty look,
His ambitious mood is bound to hook.

He spots his target in his sight,
He moves curiously in the dead of night.

His prey is blind to see the danger
That lurks, his head bowed
His tongue greedily slurps.

He licks his lips
It's almost time to taste the meat
So sweet divine.
A snap of a twig is all it takes,
For the prey to flee his escape,
He makes.

Christie Arnold (12)
The James Hornsby High School

A Ballad

There was a girl, who just started school,
She really thought she was really cool,
She posed with every step she took
And always cared about her looks.

She'd fling her rubbish in the bin
As she walked straight in
And fling her glistening hair
And acted a right cheeky mare.
She wrapped her arms around her books
And always cared about her looks.

One day she tripped and broke her nose,
Had stitches on her dainty toes,
To cover her bruises, she wore a hood,
She weren't so hooked on looking good.

She felt so sad,
She felt so bad,
She knew so well what to do.

And one day the rumours grew and grew
Until they made this girl feel blue
And from that day she never cared how she looked
She paid attention to her school books.

Latania Jones (13)
Valentines High School

CARNIVAL

Radio's all up to full blast
I know that this jam's gonna last
Carnival smell is in the air
Carnival fever everywhere.

Every kinda food is sold
Indian, African, hot or cold
Carnival smell is in the air
Carnival fever everywhere.

People dancin' in the street
Soakin' up the classy beat
Carnival smell is in the air
Carnival fever everywhere.

It doesn't matter who you are
People come from near and far
Carnival smell is in the air
Carnival fever everywhere.

Chaos, cops all block the street
But even they can feel the heat
Carnival smell is in the air
Carnival fever everywhere.

This goes on all through the night
Brightens up the London light
Carnival smell is in the air
Carnival fever everywhere.

It's now Tuesday and so
The Notting Hill market's in full flow
Carnival's over the time was mad
All enjoyed the carnival they had.

Thomas Theodore (12)
Valentines High School

MY DEAD CANARY

My canary chirped and flew about
Killed by his wife, there is no doubt
I buried my canary in the ground
In a bottle he can be found.

He used to enjoy eating his seed
He'd really like it when it was time for his feed
I buried my canary in the ground
In a bottle he can be found.

He used to enjoy having a bath
Watching would really be a laugh
I buried my canary in the ground
In a bottle he can be found.

He's probably being eaten by ants
Now he's departed it's really pants
I buried my canary in the ground
In a bottle he can be found.

Anthony Sotiriou (12)
Valentines High School

CRICKET

I was being bowled by Mac
And I hit the ball with a whack,
But now I'm out,
Without a doubt.

The ball went flying,
As I ran sighing.
But now I'm out,
Without a doubt.

The ball went past the boundary,
Into the park, it flew, soundly,
But now I'm out,
Without a doubt.

But Bill was in the park
And caught the ball with a bark.
But now I'm out,
Without a doubt.

Everyone's shouting 'Boo,'
So I'll just be thrown out of the crew.
But now I'm out,
Without a doubt.

Adil Mahboob (12)
Valentines High School

I WILL BRING MY KIDS UP DIFFERENTLY

I will bring my kids up differently
I don't want my kids to be geeks,
Or want them to be freaks
I will bring my kids up differently.

I will bring my kids up differently,
I don't want them to rob a bank,
Or to do silly pranks,
I will bring my kids up differently.

I will bring my kids up differently,
I want my boys to be clever,
Not to play with guns never . . . ever . . .
I will bring my kids up differently.

I will bring my kids up differently,
I want my girls to be smart
And not to chase after sexy boys like tarts,
I will bring my kids up differently.

Gira Patel (13)
Valentines High School

SNOW WHITE, 6 DWARVES AND A MONKEY

There was once a girl called Snow White, but I'm afraid she
                              wasn't too bright
But Snow White changed. Oh so very much, it probably
                        Was the Prince's touch.

One day she got into a huff cos her dad said she was too rough
But Snow White changed. Oh so very much, it probably
                        Was the Prince's touch.

She soon realised after her fit that she had been a silly old twit
But Snow White changed. Oh so very much, it probably
                        Was the Prince's touch.

She didn't know the forest well but somehow she found the Ritz Hotel
Soon to home the owners returned. When they saw the
                        Mess their bellies churned.

Snow White asked their names, they were: Drel and Droopy,
The outré pa-ner, there's Dippo, Dumpy, Drippy too, oh and
Dippy who acted a right fool.

Then on the mess they got working. They even found a purple gherkin
They got hungry for a pasty, so off they went to Ol' Jo Nasty.

Then Snow White said, 'Look that won't do, look it's horrid.
                              Wait that's just you.'
'Look now, we've had enough of you,' shouted the dwarves,
                              'and your BO too.'

So they tried to be rid of that pest. They would give their all
And nothing less but nothing they did do or try, that
Stubborn girl just would not die.

One day she had a KFC 'Get lost,' she said, 'Cos it's all for me,'
But Snow White changed. Oh so very much it probably
                        Was the Prince's touch.

Suddenly she choked on a bone. She said nothing but gave
                              a deep groan
Snow White fell bang! And hit the floor, the annoying
                              Snow White was no more.

The dwarves were so very happy, the monkey even wet his nappy
But it all changed, oh so very much it probably
                    Was the Prince's touch.

They had a party it was rad, then along came a young strapping lad,
'Look,' he said, 'That beautiful sight, there's no way I can't be right,'

He took her in his arms, in bliss and gave her one fat smacking
French kiss but no results! Just one more trick he gave
Snow White the Belgian Heimlich.

Suddenly Snow White did arise and opened up her big brown eyes
She saw the Prince just standing there, and so she stroked his long
Golden hair.

He placed her on his horse and rode. And they rode, and rode, and rode,
And rode, they did stay always together. And they lived
                              happily forever.

Kadon Gittens (13)
Valentines High School

SWEET POETRY

Zing, zap, wow, zingy,
Refreshers freshen you up,
Mouth-watering, eye popping,
Fantastic fizz zooms into your mouth,
Explosion of sour fun flavours into my mouth like a volcano,
Tingling, tangerling inside my mouth,
It's amazing like a magician,
An explosion of goosebumps up your neck at first suck.

Mark Fuller (11)
William Edwards School

SWEETS, GLORIOUS SWEETS

Sweets, glorious sweets!
I have millions of sweets to choose from . . .
But I choose Polos, Refreshers and Rolos.

I like the Rolos most of all,
Seas of chocolate flood into my mouth,
Then with one bite, it turns to a flavour of caramel!
The taste is like heaven!

Then you have a flavour of chocolate with
Some caramel chewed up in a bundle,
Then all of a sudden the sweet begins to
Get smaller and smaller and smaller.
Until it has disappeared, just like a puff of smoke
Once I eat one, I have to eat the rest.

Kimberley Harris (11)
William Edwards School

SWEET POETRY

Fizz, fizz, fizz, go the sweets in your mouth
Forget about the Rolos and the Polos in your mouth,
Your brain will dissolve as they rush down your throat,
So, fizz, fizz, fizz, go Refreshers in your mouth.

Steven Pasquale (11)
William Edwards School

THE POLO MINT

A peppermint is as hot as the sun,
As round as the world
Burning my mouth every time I suck it.
It feels like I'm on fire.
After a while it dissolves.
As hard as rock, smooth, fresh, nose-watering,
It is as exciting and crunchy like a biscuit
And at the point of biting the Polo mint,
It feels as if, if I take it out
My tongue will fall off.
But it is still
The best sweet ever!

Matthew Kingsland (11)
William Edwards School

POLO MINTS

P   is for the pulverising taste
O   is for the oval shape of freshness
L   is for the long-lasting mint
O   is for the oversized minty hotness

M   is for the mouth-watering urge
I   is for the illusions
N   is for the never-ending luxury
T   is for the temptation
S   is for the strongness.

Billy Harvey (11)
William Edwards School

POLO MINT

Minty, fresh, hard, refreshing,
That's what a Polo is.
It was as hot as hell
But cold like ice.
How can I make up my mind?
Crunchy, sharp, rough, sweet,
That's what a Polo is.
Hard at the start,
But soft at the end.
Well, I think I will have one more . . .

Adam Rixson (11)
William Edwards School

POLO POEM

It was like a burst of cool mint.
A tingling sensation.
Mint, like ice, getting fiery.
Sharp as a butcher's knife.
Nice and yummy.
The small sweet with the big taste.

Tony Martinez (12)
William Edwards School

POLO MINT

A Polo is a minty, refreshing sweet.
It makes your mouth smell nice and it tastes good.
If you bite it, it crunches.
After a while it dissolves.
It is smooth after the letters have gone.
You can stick your tongue through the hole.
The hotter ones make your eyes water!

Ellis Goldsmith (12)
William Edwards School

SWEET POETRY

Rolos are gooey and sticky,
They stick to your teeth like glue.
The chocolate melts in your mouth.

Sometimes they can be gaggy,
But you can never stop eating them.
They feel slimy,
But they are satisfying.

Amanda Key (11)
William Edwards School

SWEET POETRY

Rolo, Rolo, it's a very nice sweet,
With the caramel waiting for the bite,
That makes the caramel zoom out like a motorbike from the centre,
With the lovely soft and gooey centre, and the Rolo itself.
When it comes down to the last one,
Suck, suck, suck it to hell!
The smell that makes your tummy tumble in your brain,
It's chanting more, more, more . . .

Phillip Whelpton (11)
William Edwards School

REFRESHING MINT

The mint burned on my tongue,
It was eye-watering.
It smelt strong, hot, cool,
It was as hot as the huge sun.
It was as energising as a dog
And it was as white as ice.

James Warren (11)
William Edwards School

REFRESHER

The sherbet was as sherbety as a gallon of sherbet.
It filled my mouth so quickly.
It was exploding like a bomb.
The sherbet flooded my mouth.
It was sharp at times.
It was very flavoursome.

Aaron Riley (11)
William Edwards School

SWEET POETRY

As I sucked my sweet,
It exploded in my mouth.
All different sour flavours came out.
It was like a gallon of sherbet
Poured into your mouth.
Then all bits of Refresher
Tingled like sherbet in your mouth.
Then it erupted into little bits.
All little bits smashed in your mouth
Like a pane of smashed glass.

Matthew Sims (11)
William Edwards School

ROLOS

Rolos are caramel, sticky and gooey,
They flow down your throat like a pile of mud
And flood your mouth.
The taste is extremely chocolatey and chewy.
The caramel shoots up your brain
Like a bullet from a gun.
The caramel dissolves around your mouth
And sticks to your teeth and you start to dribble.
You make a puddle of chocolate.

Thomas Lyons (11)
William Edwards School

SWEET POEM

Powdery, chalky and sharp
It sizzles in my mouth
With a fruity, morish taste.
It is as crumbly as chalk,
My teeth bite it like a hawk.
The eye-popping taste makes me cringe
As the sour taste hits my brain.
The tanginess gives me a pain,
The refreshing Refresher strikes again.

Susie Limbert (11)
William Edwards School

POLO

I feel the writing on it - *Polo*
Its cool, refreshing, energising taste
Its tantalising taste makes my mouth water
Its minty taste is like mint sauce
It makes my breath feel really fresh
It dissolves in my mouth like sugar in tea
When it bite into it
Its jagged, sharp edges poke into my tongue.

Lauren Tribe (11)
William Edwards School

SWEET POETRY

The taste of the sweet is fizzy,
Go ahead and try the eye-popping sweet,
The flavour is powerful and tickles you,
But don't dare to put two in your mouth!
It is sharp when you bite into it,
It is like a Wonka Bar in your mouth.
It is crunchy and powdery,
Can you guess what it is yet?

Jason Mann (11)
William Edwards School

SWEETIE SWEET POETRY

Refreshers are like ten fizzy sherbets in your mouth.
The Refreshers are sour and sweet.
Their sweet taste is like lots of sugar and lemon mixed together.
If you look at it, it looks like a small plate.
It starts off smooth, then when I put it in my mouth it gets rough.
In my mouth it feels like an explosion.
All the flavours burst into your mouth.
You can't resist them because they're delicious.

Kaylee Tidswell (11)
William Edwards School

SWEET POETRY

Sweet, fizzy, crunchy Refresher,
Flavour burst, pressure.
Whenever I taste one, look at my mouth,
Cover your ears or hear me shout!
The flavour releases as something like Love Hearts.
It looks like a mint but with different colours.
Look at my mouth, hear me shout!
Would you like to have one?

Lesley Biggins (11)
William Edwards School

SWEET POETRY

Rolos are yummy and sticky and they get stuck to my teeth.
They are chocolatey and caramely, with a lovely chocolately taste.
The sight just fills and floods my mouth with water
And I am dribbling as they melt in my mouth.
It is better than the rest, the Rolo, just so smiley and gooey.
The chocolate is like Play Doh going down the throat from your mouth.
The Rolo is irresistible.

Keelie Adams (11)
William Edwards School

ROLOS

The Rolo was melting in my mouth,
It struck me like lightning
And I was wrapped up in my own world.
It was like an army of Rolos being beaten by me.
It was very tempting to eat another.

They smelt delicious.
They looked so tasty, I tried to keep the long lasting taste
By taking a long time to eat them.
I could hear them crunching wildly in my mouth.
I was gasping for more.

Rachel Carey (12)
William Edwards School

WHAT ABOUT SPACE?

In space there are huge stars, large planets and
a giant silence.
In space there are bleak breezes, cold surfaces
and Arctic outsides.
In space there are low hollows, whispering people
and tranquil booms far away.

In rockets there are loud rackets of bursting air.
The comets go by scalding the surroundings
and the middle's red-hot.
Noisy, shooting stars, wringing, crashing and shouting.

Jessica Law (12)
William Edwards School

SPACE

I wish I lived on the moon,
Amongst the twinkling stars,
I'd watch the planets every day,
Jupiter, Saturn and Mars.

I'd walk along the Milky Way
And dance on silvery beams.
I'd visit friendly aliens,
Seen only in my dreams.

I'd glide through the galaxies,
With space my only friend.
Comets would go flashing by
Until reaching journey's end.

I'd wave at moonbound astronauts,
How happy I would be,
To be all alone in space,
Just the moon, stars and me!

Holly Dawson (12)
William Edwards School

A POEM ABOUT SPACE

Stars: I look above and see a star
That is really far
Above my head.
As I lie in bed.
I see them every day
And know they're so far away.

Planets: All those planets, in the air
Especially the sun which makes a flare.
Mars and Saturn,
Make a pattern
And the moon at night
Makes a bright light.

Astronauts: There are lots of astronauts,
What happens if they make an astrofault?
Do they shout? Do they cry?
If they're unlucky, do they die?
'Houston, Houston, we have a problem!'
'Yes Apollo, it's a faulty modem!'

Aaron Milan-Vega (12)
William Edwards School

SPACE

Space the final frontier
NASA's been there
So why can't all of us
Maybe in the future we can.

Films have been made about space
Star Wars, a massive hit
TV programmes also are big
Such as Star Trek.

Many mission have been done
And we have learnt from these
Could there be life on Mars?
A smart computer could tell us.

Space is a new adventure
To enjoy.
It is amazing!

Michael Guerrero (12)
William Edwards School

LOST IN SPACE

You take off like a bullet being fired from a gun
Then you're in space, the view outside is glorious
The sky around you is a beautiful deep blue
The clouds below look like whirls of paint
And the sky above is ebony with sprinkled stars
You see a large, bright star so bright it hurts to look at it
You feel the heat hitting you like a bolt of lightning
Then your spaceship lands, you get out and bounce around
Then you fall in a moon crater!
You are thinking what will you do
Then you realise that you are lost in space
How will you get home?
Will you?

Ben Murphy (12)
William Edwards School

A POEM ABOUT SPACE

Cor! I'm in space
I can see all the planets
Look Dave, there's the moon
And the sun

It's nice and peaceful
The moon is enormous
Look at the stars
Yeah and look there's Mars

There's ET over there
Where, where?
Only joking

It's scorching in here
Hang on, I'll open the window
No you fool
What! What!
Are you stupid?
No, you must be,
Getting in the spaceship with me.

Bradley Mumford (12)
William Edwards School

SPACE

5, 4, 3, 2, 1, 0, blast-off
Sweating hot as the screaming engine drives the humungous rocket
To the scorching planet of Mars
Frozen as I look back at my home planet
I listen for a noise but it's complete silence
As I am taken though a tiny bunch of red-hot stars
In the distance I can see a ball of molten lava
As I approach the flaming ball I boil in my suit
Eventually I'm past
I look around the rocket then something catches my eye
It's a meteorite and it's heading straight for me
Suddenly I wish I was back at home
Bang . . . it was just a fabulous dream.

Nathanael Bareham (12)
William Edwards School

SPACE

In the dark, dark sky
The stars shine brightly
Like little diamonds
Far, far away

Shooting stars
Flying in the sky
Zooming past planets
But where do they come from?

Are there living creatures on planets
Millions of miles from here?
Will we ever know?

Will we ever land on planets spinning round?
Are they hot?
Are they cold?
Only time can tell.

That is what I think of space.

Harshabir Bal (12)
William Edwards School

SPACE

The rocket took off
the stars glistened across the sky
the sun was shining with a terrific amount of light
with a planet around you couldn't hear a sound.
But suddenly across the sky a comet sped through
the air, shimmering as it went
The air was thin and no gravity was present
Bouncing across the moon was the astronaut
bobbing and weaving as he went
across the silent night sky
Night-fire red to be precise was the colour of the sky.
The moon is the future!

Thomas Street (12)
William Edwards School

MY SPACE POEM

A tranquil, frigid galaxy lie still,
no atmosphere,
silence deafening,
an uproar sounds,
aliens march up and over planets,
drumming,
a shriek,
the planets begin to vibrate,
no oxygen,
another cry,
slowly aliens begin to die,
the sun's light no longer shines,
no solar energy,
all living creatures remain still,
dead.
A galaxy of creatures who once existed has disappeared,
into what?

Claire England (12)
William Edwards School

SPACE

Astronauts go into space,
It looks like a very magical place.
All the sparkling stars in the sky,
Why they're there I don't know why.
I believe that in the past,
A great explosion made the stars.
The sun's up there so hot and bright,
That's where Earth gets all its light.
Are there aliens up there? Nobody knows,
If they were, would they be friends or foes?
Astronauts go into space,
It looks like a very magical place.

Jodi Cooper (12)
William Edwards School

SPACE ODDITY

There was a man from space who had a funny face,
He leapt to the stars while eating a Mars
and fell back down like a comet.
He tried getting into another dimension,
but I wouldn't like to mention that the Milky Way
and Mars needed his attention.

The alien was light years away,
because he was waiting for Independence Day.
While lost in space there was no air.
He met ET and the Men In Black
and asked them why they were coming back.

The alien returned to Mars and then went to the moon
he spoke to some astronauts who said they'll be back soon.
He went with them back to the shuttle
and watched the solar eclipse and the astronaut said
'Oh no, there's no alien ships.'

Paul Jones (12)
William Edwards School